MEN

MID-COURSE CORRECTION

Gordon MacDonald

THOMAS NELSON PUBLISHERS
Nashville

Copyright © 2000 by Gordon MacDonald

Published in Nashville, Tennessee, by Thomas Nelson, Inc.

Library of Congress Cataloging-in-Publication Data

MacDonald, Gordon, 1939-
    Mid-course correction / Gordon MacDonald.
        p.   cm.
    Includes bibliographical references.
    ISBN 0-7852-7841-9 (hardcover)
    1. Christian life. I. Title.
    BV4501.2.M2268 2000
    248.8'4—dc21   99-088448
                                                                CIP

Printed in the United States of America

1 2 3 4 5 6   BVG   05 04 03 02 01 00

To my brother whom I love, David W. MacDonald

I'd have been a lot nicer to you when we were kids if I'd known how much of a friend and encourager you would be when we grew up.

CONTENTS

CONTENTS

ACKNOWLEDGMENTS

Every book I write is really a joint effort with my wife, Gail, who reads every word several times over and offers insight and perspective. These are times when our mutual journey in faith always gets a push forward as we spend literally hours talking over what is going on the page. Our partnership in life is a precious solidarity as it nears forty years in length.

***

Thanks to my publisher Victor Oliver (Oliver Nelson), with whom I have had a relationship (and friendship) that has flourished for nearly twenty-five years.

And thanks to Cindy Blades (Thomas Nelson), who has shepherded this book through its editing and production.

Behind these two people are scores of people who work very hard to make a book a reality. We never get to meet, but I want them to know that I am humbled and grateful for all they do with such excellence.

VITAL OPTIMISM

In a new book entitled *The First World War*, military historian John Keegan makes this comment about the war's most horrific battle: "The Somme (together with the battle of Ypres in July, 1917 where 70,000 British were killed and 170,000 wounded) marked the end of an age of vital optimism in British life that has never been recovered." The last part of that sentence stirred something in my mind, and I found myself thinking about a society that had, for more than a hundred years, enjoyed a wild run of vital optimism and then, overnight, according to Keegan, lost it. And worse: *never recovered it.*

Think about it! One terrible battle with catastrophic losses, and the cultural momentum (centuries in the making) of a great nation is arrested, dissipated.

I'm drawn to Keegan's term *vital optimism.* It describes a quality of spirit possessed by a community or a person where there is a persuasion that the best is yet to be. Whatever the past, the future will be better. Nineteenth-century Victorian England really believed that. From such a spirit come increasing excitement, incentive, and the love of nobler purposes. Nineteenth-century Victorian England had all of that.

A loss, then, of vital optimism suggests the opposite: melancholy, disincentive, and a general sense of resignation. I hear Keegan saying that this became the prevailing mood in England *after* 1917.

What Keegan calls *vital optimism,* I call *hope:* the confident expectation that history is going somewhere and that God, our Creator and Redeemer, is powerfully directing it. Without such vital optimism or hope, life is, to say the least, quite troublesome.

I have known many people who, after a personal struggle of some kind (proportionately similar to Britain's tragedy at the Somme), have lost *their* vital optimism. A man comes to mind who was suddenly terminated from a high-level job. No one, including him, could have foreseen such a possibility. He was devastated; he never really recovered from the shock. Now, more than a dozen years later, he remains stuck in cynicism and bitterness, and as far as I can see, his life is going nowhere.

A woman, whose intellect I greatly admired and who often provided sound advice to me on matters of church administration, dropped me a note one day and said she was leaving our congregational community. It wasn't that we had done anything wrong. She had just lost her enthusiasm for what we were into. Nothing was working for her any longer. From being very much at the center of our people, she dropped off the edge and disappeared.

But why speak of others when I can recall a time I lost *my* vital optimism? I once tasted a version of the dissipated spirit. The matter of hope, that there is a future, is not an academic subject for me.

Unless one is born into a life where the circumstances are unbearably gloomy and disheartening (and more than a few have been), vital optimism seems a given during childhood and youth. From our earliest days we hear that we can do anything, go anywhere, and achieve any goal if we are willing to work hard enough. And this wonderful, reasonably true myth keeps us going for some time.

But reality can chip away at this myth and erode our dreams, and by the time we are in our late thirties, the fight to retain any kind of vital optimism is fierce. From living life built on great expectations, we gravitate toward a life built on little more than obligation. I have often smiled at the comment made by my friend who said, "I started life thinking I'd hit a home run every time I came to bat. Now I just want to get through the game without getting beaned on the head by the ball."

Biblical people (those who are committed to building their lives around the teaching of Scripture and the Christ who is at its center) are usually characterized, at least among themselves, as having a unique kind of vital optimism. They tell one another that there is a world to change, that people by the millions are anxious to hear what they have to say (if they'll only say it), that there is a supernatural power capable of overcoming any conceivable human limitation.

Biblical people like to remind one another that, in the words of a nineteenth-century notable, "the world has yet to see what God can do through one person totally committed to Him." I know that when I was a young and very impressionable Christ-follower, that comment generated a lot of anticipation in me; it kept me going for a long time.

But it was more than renovating the world. We came to believe that if we pushed *ourselves* hard enough, we could achieve a certain level of saintliness, a coveted spiritual maturity (self-control, humility, contentment, and a wisdom like unto that of our Christian heroes). To us, vital optimism meant a belief that we could tap into a resource of zeal and energy (the power of the Holy Spirit) that might make us unusually fruitful. And beyond all of this, we sincerely anticipated reaching a state of love for God and an experience of seamless communion with Him.

These were then, and remain today, splendid aspirations. But they were and are also illusive. At just the moment when you were tempted to think you'd advanced in any one of these areas of growth, something happened to suggest that there were yet miles to go. Then when it was almost too late, you learned that you never really "arrive" in matters like these. You never earn the designation "spiritually mature" quite like you receive a Ph.D. degree. Or to express it in another way, if you are given a plaque for outstanding humility, they'll take it away if you hang it on your wall.

There are many, among the biblical people, who report that they have experienced some or all of these qualities. I would certainly like to think that in my years of following after Christ, I've grown a bit. I met a man in Holland who told me with a straight face that he had managed not to sin for twelve years. And he didn't seem like a nut either. But he was an exception.

When they are together, biblical people love to talk about their enthusiasm for faith. Some even write books or articles about it or go on the road and offer seminars and speak at conferences so that others can emulate them. I have read many of the books, and I've attended a few of the conferences. In my younger years I often went away with a kind of excitement that I now compare to a "sugar high." The feeling didn't last long, and the letdown was disappointing. So I have reservations about some of the promises we make and the intentions we declare because it seems that we try to *talk things into reality* when we aren't actually experiencing them.

As I implied earlier, in the early days of my spiritual journey, I had plenty of vital optimism. If I did lose it for a time, it probably happened in 1987. That was the year I had to publicly confess to a time of personal failure in my life. It was difficult to watch the details spill out across the network of media and personal connections that the religious community maintains, and I learned that, in the eyes of some, one is only as good as his last battle. And like the British of 1917, I had lost big time.

At the time the wisest thing was to go into seclusion, and that is exactly what my wife, Gail, and I did. We remained there, in blessed, restorative quiet, for almost two years until gracious people asked us back.

In the early months of that two-year blackout period, I faced the fact that I had lost an enormous amount of hope. Known before as a visionary, I no longer had a vision. Regarded by some as being an encourager to the young, I no longer had encouragement to give. I was altogether empty and disheartened by what I had done and what people thought of me.

The diaries of American author Leonard Michaels were recently published under the title *Time Out of Mind*. Leonard's life was not altogether a pretty one, and he recognized that. At one point in his writing, when he has assayed the consequences of three failed marriages and estranged children, he says of himself, "I seem almost to contemplate a stranger. He [speaking of himself] did and said things I'd never do, never say. I want to claim he isn't me." Still, he observes wryly, since the diary obviously reflects his writing style and his handwriting, "[I have] no choice but to conclude that I am, in a very personal sense, that man."

I understand what Leonard Michaels is saying because in my dark days I wanted to join the crowd who pointed their fingers and shook their heads and say, "You're absolutely right; I don't like me either." That's what loss of enthusiasm for life can sound like.

The poet Ed Sissman once wrote:

> Men past forty
> Get up nights
> Look out at city lights
> And wonder why life is so long
> And where they made the wrong turn.

I've been there!

To lose one's spirit of hope is a terrible thing. But it happens. And not to a small percentage of us, but to a huge percentage of us. When and if it happens, the question becomes, *Can I ever retrieve the spirit again?* In my times of gloomy reverie in 1987, I was not sure. Slowly, I came to a moment when I determined to find out.

When I think of people who fall into the category of having lost their vital optimism, I think of folk like these:

- They are disappointed in themselves and in the direction their lives are moving.

- They have been immersed (in good faith) in all the noise of organized religious life, but they have lost track of what is really important and what God might actually expect of them.

- They are well aware that the world is changing, that life has been sped up, that their options are exploding in number, but their faith is not keeping up with it all and has become obsolete.

- They feel that they are close to becoming stuck; they know they need to change, but they feel that it may be impossible to do so now.

- They intuit that there is something deeper, a more satisfying way of life than they have now.

I imagine these people sitting in the room as I put these thoughts together. I want most to connect with these people.

In writing this book (the most difficult of all my books), I will try to make several things converge in order to provoke thought. There will be, I hope, some fresh ideas. Then there will be some familiar stories from the Bible, which I hope to retell in a way that will challenge you to see your biblical life in new ways. Scattered throughout all of this: a few stories from various sources and my experiences with other people. As you will see, I love stories.

Finally, I want to take the risk of disclosing a bit of my spiritual journey up to this sixtieth year of my life. Wherever I think it will be useful, I will not hesitate to share my life and thoughts-in-progress. I'm old enough now to share the good *and* the bad without overly worrying what people will think. And by the way, I'm far enough down the road now not to have angst about venturing to the edge and trying out a few experimental ideas from which, one day, I may have to back away and say, "Hey, I wrote that when I was a much younger man." I have to assume that you will think with appropriate discrimination.

Occasionally in the writing, I'll blend in the stories of others who have either given me permission or whose experience I have masked so completely that privacy is not compromised.

What do I hope will come out the other end of my writing? First, a provocation for biblical people to rethink what it means to possess a vital optimism best defined by the biblical writers. And, second, a renewed conviction that one's life can, if necessary, experience a radical change of direction, spiritual depth, and effectiveness. As I see it, three great themes provide a foundation for all life-change, three things not adequately addressed in the usual run of things:

1. *The hidden purposes of God,* which require obedience, trust, and a sense of stewardship. The key question: What do I really believe? The operative word: *leave.*

2. *The hidden life of the biblical person,* which is reshaped by the influence of Jesus Christ. The key question: Who am I? The operative word: *follow.*

3. *The hidden recognitions of heaven,* which come to those who extend themselves without reservation in the cause of building the kingdom. The key question: What could I accomplish? The operative word: *reach.*

If I were asked to reduce the nature of the biblical life to three words, they would be *leave, follow,* and *reach.* For me, everything can fit under one of these categories. However, our modern culture (the religious and the nonreligious) seems to have little comprehension of or inclination to these three themes.

Everything I've written here (themes, stories, quotes) is built on one central thought that, in pursuit of a bit of freshness, I have identified by using a space-age term: *mid-course correction.* Synonyms for the term are *life-change, conversion, transformation, renewal,* and *reorganization.*

The best and simplest definition I can give of the term *mid-course correction* is "the process that introduces biblically based life-change to a man or woman who has lost vital optimism."

I am fresh from a conversation with a man in his mid-forties. His second marriage has imploded, and the chances are iffy at best that it will be healed. He has completed a handful of years with a well-known financial company and has been reasonably successful. If God wills, he has thirty, forty more years to live. But there is a despair, a blank stare, if you please, in his demeanor. The brain is in motion; the personality is rather pleasing. He is a good person. But the vital optimism is gone. Do these seeming contradictions in my description make sense?

This is a real person I am describing. He has given me permission to write these words. He understands that he is not unique, that his search for a rebirth of life is a common one to many others.

When I ask him where he thinks his center of gravity for success is to be found, he admits that the perception of success has been the all-important issue. "I think I can sum it all up for you in this way," he says. "Each morning I go to our executive dining room, and I sit at breakfast with a half dozen men who are at the top of this company. I feel good sitting with them. I like to be seen with them. The moments at the table make me feel as if I've arrived.

"But then, when breakfast is over and we all get up, the six of them walk together toward the elevators, and I walk alone behind them. When we reach the elevators, they all get on one elevator, and I get on another. It's at that moment that I realize: I'm not one of them. It was only a momentary illusion."

When my friend is finished with his story, I make this suggestion. "Why not," I ask, "designate a forty-five-day period during which you will dabble in studying the architecture of your whole life in order to set it on an entirely new course?"

"I could do that," he says. "How would I get started?"

"Three words," I answer. He actually writes them down as I identify them: *leave, follow,* and *reach.* And then I tell him about this book.

MID-COURSE CORRECTION:
How This Book Got Its Title

I have seen the movie *Apollo 13* several times. A scene halfway through the film never fails to inspire me. While headed toward a rendezvous with the moon, the *Apollo 13*, piloted by Jim Lovell (played by Tom Hanks), sustains a crippling explosion. The words "Houston . . . we have a problem" have become part of the American idiomatic vocabulary in recent years. It's a way of saying, "Something is wrong here."

When the crew and the ground controllers assess the damage caused by the explosion, it becomes evident that a moon landing will no longer be possible. The mission must be scrapped. The only priority is to bring the astronauts back to earth safely, and the odds are not good that this can happen.

The primary problem is that the *Apollo 13* is off course as it comes around the moon and heads back toward Earth. A carefully timed and executed mid-course correction is essential, or the three astronauts aboard will die when the *Apollo 13* enters the earth's atmosphere at a wrong angle and burns to a cinder. But such a correction is no small thing to make happen given other problems, such as minimal electrical power and unreliable computers.

After some frenzied but brilliant brainstorming, there is a remarkable exercise in teamwork between the astronauts and the people at the Johnson Center in Houston. A thirty-nine-second "burn" of the thrusters is attempted, and the tricky process of getting *Apollo 13* on the correct track is completed to perfection. The result: a safe splashdown in the Pacific Ocean.

In the world of space exploration, a mid-course correction is a refinement in the direction of a space vehicle so that it will reach its intended destination. In this book *mid-course correction* refers to the process of regenerating, redirecting, and refining the spiritual life of the biblical person. A rather expansive process, I'd say. No small matter.

Tennyson had a mid-course correction in life in mind when he wrote:

> Oh, for a new man to arise in me,
> That the man I am may cease to be.

He can be referring only to a revision of life that begins at the core of one's life—we call it the heart or soul—and works outward. Biblical people refer to this as *conversion,* the starting point of all lasting life-change. Conversion in this sense is built upon the conviction that something is and has been terribly awry in the spiritual center of every human being since the very first generation. Something akin to a rebirth is needed, and that can be accomplished only through a work initiated by God. Without this amending of life, there will be a marked tendency for everything else in the human experience to be slightly (or not so slightly) out of kilter. Like an off-course space vehicle, the human being can experience only drift.

Conversion implies the problem of sin, a spiritual disease that distorts reality and leads to a defiance of God's laws and principles of life. So, to repeat myself, *conversion* is seen as the grand corrective.

Biblical people believe that *conversion* always begins with an encounter between a person and God. Frequently, they like to argue over who initiates this encounter, but the fact is that they are in agreement this far: In conversion a supernatural convergence occurs. The apostle Paul expressed it in the idea of becoming a *new creation;* Jesus spoke of it as being *born again.* These were attempts to say that *life can change and should change, begin, as it were, all over again.*

I have always been fascinated with the question of *how* people change. It was a subject on my mind when I was a child, and I heard the first stories from the Bible accompanied with the invitation to "receive Jesus into my heart." And I accepted that invitation, raised my hand, went to the front of the room, put my name on the card many times in subsequent years even though I'd heard that once was enough. But those invitations were so compelling, my desire to please so great, my growing sense of guilt so real that receiving Jesus into my heart more than once seemed the prudent thing to do. I have no doubt that original responses to these invitations were far more driven to please people than God, but I also have no doubt that something deep in my life's interior was beginning to reach out toward God nonetheless.

When I was a teenager, I began to see these things from a multi-layered perspective. At the deepest level I was still inviting Jesus into my life (although less frequently) when the pressure was on. But I was seeking other kinds of changes also. Presenting the appropriate appearance, acting "cool," using the correct language, going to the right places with the right people—these were all forms of personal transformation, even if they were superficial at best.

No alteration of life seemed too great if it would provide access to the peer group or win the favor of some girl whom I found attractive. I was prepared to submit to virtually any kind of change in order to be accepted, if not admired. Not much to brag about there, but you understand.

3

In my early twenties I finally reached a defining moment about my faith. In the summer of 1959, I prayed to Jesus, saying that I wanted to offer Him my life so that, as much as possible, all of its details might be organized around Him. I would follow Him, I said, to the best of my conscious abilities. Somehow, I never felt the need to make that declaration again. I reaffirmed it many times. But unlike in my younger days, I became satisfied that I'd been heard. The issue of overall life-direction had been settled as far as I was concerned, and I would now assume that He, Jesus, would "call" if I'd missed anything.

Mid-course corrections of another kind were necessary as I met my wife, Gail, for whom I was prepared to do anything. When I became a pastor, when I became a father, when I became responsible for a sizable staff of coworkers—all this called upon me to make modifications of life that might lead to greater effectiveness or greater integrity of one kind or another. When I made stupid choices, when I uncovered substandard patterns of thought and behavior, when friends and critics rebuked me, I sought more ways to upgrade the quality of my life. Many of them stuck; others did not and had to be restarted again and again.

Now I cross the line of the sixtieth year of my life. And I still see ways in which I must change direction. In character, habits, personal conduct. This is okay because I've become newly convinced that the refining of self is a key to a long and vital life. This is what it means to be on the growing edge. Not just to acquire more things, or do more things, or know more things, but to be a genuinely noble person, to be a better companion and friend, to serve with greater humility and effectiveness, to love God more fully.

In the introduction I made reference to John Keegan, who writes of a whole nation losing its vital optimism because of a couple of devastating battles. I write, keeping in mind the many who feel as if they have lost their vital optimism, their joy of faith, because of the battles in their lives. With battle-scarred people such as these as my companions, I should like to think aloud about what it takes to make life new.

Perhaps the people most interested in this topic will be those who have (as they say) taken bullets, failed, fallen, screwed up in life. They think of mid-course correction as a matter of coming back and wonder if they can. Can anyone escape the patterns and attitudes that get us into trouble? *Can anyone truly change?*

Many are tempted to believe that the answer is no, that there comes some critical moment in life when the development of a deeper, broader, more spirited life is no longer possible. And without thinking through the ramifications of their perception, they give up and abandon all hope of further transformation. Which, I say respectfully, is kind of stupid, certainly out of sync with what I hear Jesus, the Author of life-change, saying.

I like the symbolism of *mid-course correction*. In this book I'll use the term a lot to refer to the ways we seek to initiate change in our lives at any age and in any circumstance. Journey with me through the noisy thinking of these chapters and then come to your own conclusions. What does *mid-course correction* look like to you?

Chapter 1

SEEKING THE STRAIGHT PATH

Dante Alighieri, a fourteenth-century Florentine poet, was thirty-five years old when he gave the world *The Divine Comedy*, considered a standard in the repertoire of Western literature. He wrote it during a defining moment in his life. Everything was in a state of meltdown.

Dante had been on the losing side of a failed revolution, and as a result he had been exiled from his beloved city of Florence. He knew that if he ever returned, he would be put to death. The result? A life suddenly flooded with enormous uncertainty, doubt, fear. For a man drowning in disappointment, it was time for mid-course correction.

You discern his state of mind when you read the first words of *The Divine Comedy*:

> In the middle of the journey of our [my] life
> I came to my senses in a dark forest,
> for I had lost the straight path. (H. R. Huse, trans.)

With these lines Dante commenced an imaginative literary journey that explored the regions of purgatory, hell, and heaven, and high-lighted the lives of people, some out of ancient history and some (friends and adversaries) who were Dante's contemporaries. Read *The Divine Comedy*, and you'll be grateful that you didn't make Dante's enemies list. If you did make it, it meant that your life's secrets were exposed and brought to judgments and punishments designed and prescribed by a very creative and vindictive poet.

But the real issue of *The Divine Comedy* is Dante himself. Vital optimism was ebbing away. "I came to *my* senses in a dark forest." These words describe something of a personal awakening: eyes opening to things either forgotten or not seen before. The man is telling us that he is preparing *to rearrange his life.*

Dante's dark forest was not a literal forest but a figurative one. His forest existed deep in the interior life. To borrow his vivid word picture, I'd like to suggest that all of us, from time to time, find ourselves in dark forests. Forests of our own making or products of situations over which we have no control.

The picture of Dante lost in a dark forest reminds me of Jim Lovell and his crew coming around from the back side of the moon and heading back toward earth on the wrong track. *Dark forests and mid-course corrections:* the former, the desperate situation; the latter, the potential solution. They're word pictures from two worlds more than six centuries apart.

I've never been in space, but I have known a literal dark forest. I once spent two weeks in a primitive Indian village. One morning the chief of the village invited me to join a hunting party bent on finding a wild boar seen earlier at sunrise. Two other white men (also visitors to the village) joined me as we walked and jogged behind the Indians about two miles into the forest, a steamy-hot, semi-dark, absolutely pathless jungle. Then, suddenly, we were faced with a medical emergency when one of the white men went into a diabetic coma.

It became necessary for me to return to the village to summon help. But how could I find my way back? The men in the hunting party had left us to pursue their prey. The only one among us who knew how to find the village was an Indian boy who could not have been more than ten or eleven years of age.

Quickly, he was instructed in his own tongue to lead me back to other English-speaking people who could bring help. He apparently got the message because he began to run. "Just follow him," someone instructed me.

I remember wishing that the kid had known the difference between swift walking and sprinting. He didn't. Believe me when I say that we shattered the world record for the two-mile dash (I consciously use this word). For him it was a casual jog, but for me it meant running for my life. As I tried to keep up with him, I kept wondering what "Slow down!" or "I'm dying!" or "I've fallen, and I can't get up!" might sound like in his language.

As I said, the jungle had no paths that I could discern, no directional signs, of course, and only marginal light under a dense cover of trees. It was, indeed, the dark forest of Dante's imagination, and if I had become separated from my young guide, I would have wandered about totally lost until something bad happened. Then, too, if he had injured himself, there would have been nothing I could have done to save us. There was no straight path. There was really no path at all.

Fortunately, a straight path to the village was clearly fixed in the boy's head, and we made it to our destination and fulfilled our mission. I have generally shied away from long-distance runs (especially with kids) ever since.

I described the experience only because it firmed up in my mind the literal feeling of exhaustion and helplessness, what it's like to feel great danger, and how important it is to keep up with one who knows the path. Many years later, in 1987, when I was in a spiritual dark forest, I recalled those moments in the Amazon jungle and saw several parallels in the experiences.

Many are the conversations and correspondences I've had with men and women who have lost the straight path in their lives. I guess that more than a few of these connections happen because some people know that I am no stranger to dark-forest moments. Having read one of my books, *Rebuilding Your Broken World,* they call and begin the conversation like this: "I need to tell you that I'm a broken-world person."

In another place I have written of a memorable conversation I had with a man who, in the context of this thinking, could not have been in a darker forest.

He called to ask if he might come by for a talk. When he arrived, it was evident that he was highly agitated because a job he sought had been given to another. I gained the impression that he had persuaded himself that the job would be his. And now, that expectation had been shattered.

He recounted how he got the news, and as he did, it became increasingly clear that larger, longer-term issues about his whole life, not just this job, were surfacing. This event was the proverbial straw that broke the camel's back. There wasn't an ounce of vital optimism evident in his life. Soon he was weeping, strong wrenching sobs, and a great, great inner sorrow began to disclose itself.

After sitting quietly for a while, I said, "Tell me where these tears are coming from."

When he could gain enough control, he responded, "I'm just so disappointed. So disappointed."

"Disappointed in what?" I whispered. But deep in my intuitive self, I already knew the answer.

"In everything. I've had dreams and high hopes all my life. And nothing . . . nothing has ever turned out the way I expected. Jobs fall through; friendships don't make it; I feel as if I've flunked as a husband and father. My Christian life stinks. Nothing . . . nothing works." In a brief burst of words, he had offered up his perception of a whole life.

I've recounted this unforgettable conversation because it has powerfully marked me. Not many days after we talked, this man died. Suddenly! They said he died of natural causes, but I've always believed he died of a broken heart. I genuinely liked him and wished I could have been a better pastor and friend. I wonder if I could have helped him recover his vital optimism in a way that would have lifted him from his fever of despair. Looking back upon that talk, I realize that he never spoke of anything that suggested the hope of personal transformation; he apparently saw no such possibility. And when one sees no such possibility, one faces only despair and perhaps the ultimate broken heart.

If I could get a second shot at that conversation, I would like to have offered my friend more hope. I should have dared him to take a hard look at himself and ask if it wasn't time for a personal overhaul of life. Would he have taken the bait and sought such a transformation? I don't know.

I do know that I was thinking of him a few years later when I spent a day climbing in the White Mountains of New Hampshire with a man who was facing a similar package of sadnesses. He, too, was disappointed in just about everything in his life: his lack of character and moral fiber, his choice of career, the quality of his marriage, his apathy about the future. After I had listened for an hour as he described these things, I stopped and looked at him. The best thing I could think to say was, "I don't know what to tell you except that you need one heck of a conversion!" In truth I longed for a lightning bolt that would sear his interior life, eradicate his past, redirect his future.

Perhaps I was venting more frustration than anything. But I believe so strongly in the power of God to change the direction of people lost in their dark forests that I had to blurt it out and hope that he would get the message.

John, writer of the fourth Gospel, recorded a conversation between Jesus and an unnamed woman. Their encounter happened at a place called Jacob's well on the edge of a Samaritan town, Sychar. Jesus, tired from travel, was resting; the woman had come to get water. The subject matter of their discussion swiftly moved from surface to depth as Jesus, using water as a word picture, introduced her to the possibility of spiritual life-change: "The water I give . . . will become a spring of water welling up to eternal life."

The difference in their perspectives was immediately made plain. She assumed He spoke of a kind of magic water that assuaged physical thirst. He was speaking of a change that only He could affect deep within her being, which was something she badly needed.

Her life was characterized by a kind of promiscuity (perhaps the only way she could see to support herself), and she was, most likely, a social (and religious) outcast in the village where she lived. If anyone had lost the straight path, it was she.

"Come, see a man who told me everything I ever did. Could this be the Christ?" she called out to the people of Sychar when she returned home. Clearly, the light of the character and the words of Jesus had penetrated her own dark forest. Working backward from these words, you can easily assume that the conversation at the well had been fruitful, that she had come to realize the possibility of personal transformation under His guidance.

The transformation in her being must have been so obvious that the people of Sychar became convinced that it was worth the time to return with her to where Jesus was still sitting. And before long they had all joined her in His presence to hear more about the kind of life-change that restores vital optimism.

"Many believed in him," John wrote, and Jesus ended up remaining with them for an extra two days.

"We know who this man really is," they were heard to say later. "We know that this man really is the Savior of the world" (see John 4:1–42).

I call up the story because it is one of numerous biblical references to transformation of life. And it features people who are well aware that they are in dark forests, having lost a straight path, and that the way out resides in the words and deeds of Jesus.

I have known a man with a remarkable sense of humor. I loved him (still do) for many reasons, among them the fact that he made us all laugh. But it was many years into the friendship when I became aware that there were significant defects, kept very secret in his life, that had been successfully camouflaged by the skillful use of humor. With everything a joke and everyone laughing, it was a cinch that no one would suspect that anything was amiss in the deeper parts of his life. Perhaps, and I do not know this for sure, he even used this marvelous gift to keep himself from suspecting how much was wrong in the deeper parts. When he came to his dark-forest moments, we were all astonished but shouldn't have been. The humor, however enjoyable, had been a cover over more substantial and tragic realities, for him and us, and we should have been sensitive to what was going on.

What my friend did with humor, others of us have done through our work. In the days before I found myself in the darkest of all my darkened forests, I accelerated my workload to an absurd intensity. With all the surface intention of doing good, I traveled the country speaking and consulting and enjoying the affirmation of people wherever I went. Many interpreted my apparent zeal as a sign of my commitment to God and to ministry. And there was indeed a lot of that. But the greater truth, as I see it in retrospect, was that I was on the run. Running, you could say, from the necessity of facing myself, running from the truth, from the inevitable occasion when things about me that I preferred not to face might see the light of day.

What my friend did with humor and I did with work, others have done through acquiring things, or playing incessantly, or pursuing a chain of lovers, or withdrawing into self-justifying hostility and anger. My work, which has caused me to engage many people on a very personal basis, has allowed me to see multiple examples of all of these. Perhaps the last on the list is the most horrifying to me. I have watched several men in their eighties who are bitter and reclusive. They have few friends and manage, sooner or later, to alienate the ones they do have. All because they are unwilling to acknowledge the need to "know themselves" or (using Dante's words) to come to their senses.

DISINTEGRATION

I see dark-forest moments when people come to their senses. These happen under three general conditions. I call the first *personal disintegration*. Life falls apart under the weight of consequences from destructive choices that bring the journey to a screeching halt. Losses through death, serious illness, financial reverse. Think of any bewildering occasion that disrupts life and causes a disintegration of life's structure. Vital optimism is gone.

Not far from where we live at Peace Ledge, New Hampshire, is a huge speedway where cars race at speeds exceeding 160 miles per hour. I can't think of a better gift to give my grandson, Lucas, than an afternoon at the track as the various drivers practice and then run their qualifying laps for placement in the weekend races.

The other day we watched a driver hit the wall, as they say. His magnificent racing machine disintegrated; parts flew all over the place. Because the driver's compartment was well designed, and because he was dressed in protective cover, he received no serious injury. But the car ceased being a car. And the specter of this accident caused me to think of the numerous lives, not excluding my own, that have hit the wall, causing disintegration. Reputation, career, relationships, wealth destroyed.

That was what Dante was getting at. Life had utterly fallen apart for him. He'd joined the wrong side.

On the very day that I write this chapter, a phone call has come from a pastor in another part of North America. Some months ago he had engaged in a series of conversations with a woman who had come to his office seeking assistance. As the conversations ensued, an emotional connection grew between the two of them. What had originally started with handshakes of greeting became hugs of affection. And then, as the weeks passed, the hugs became a doorway to other forms of physical demonstration until there was sexual involvement. All this he recounts to me in a matter of minutes.

An attempt to break off this relationship had gone poorly (as they almost always do), and the other person has now informed the board of the church of what has happened. Today, he says, he must stand before that same board and acknowledge his culpability, inform his wife of what has happened, and face the almost certain reality that his life as a minister, a spiritual leader of people, is over. This is, to say the least, a terrible, terrible day. As he describes what is about to happen, his voice breaks, and he begins to weep. He curses himself for his stupidity, and he wonders aloud about the future. What can he do?

This is disintegration, a moment in the dark forest when one realizes that life will never again be the same. I know, perhaps better than he, that there is hope for tomorrow. That he can come through this and emerge in the light a better, deeper, more useful man than he has been up until this time. But when you're in the dark forest, when you've lost your vital optimism about a future in God's hand, that's hard to believe.

DISAPPOINTMENT

A second occasion that triggers dark-forest moments is what I call *personal disappointment.* We saw an extreme example of that a page or two back.

My observation is that many of us come to dark-forest moments when we look at the major sectors of our lives and conclude that what is there falls short of what we'd anticipated when we started. A marriage has lasted, but the relationship has run out of energy. It is tired. No longer are two people gladdened by each other's presence; no longer is there the impetus to know each other at greater depth or serve each other with greater enthusiasm.

A job, once challenging and filled with promise, is now little more than a job. One goes to it each day counting the years before it can be left behind in retirement.

A faith, once vibrant, filled with a vision of personal growth and service, has now gone flat. It no longer feeds the soul, and there is an emptiness, a hollowness within that is never quite filled.

"What's your book about?" a new acquaintance asked.

I dread a question like that because the responses from people are never quite satisfactory to a writer who is quietly putting his soul on paper and feeling more than a little vulnerable.

"I'm writing about the corrections people seek to make in their lives when they hit a wall."

"A wall?"

"Yeah," I said. I told him about the conversation on disappointment that I described earlier in this chapter and then said, "A lot of people tend to come to a major break point in life where they are quite disappointed about a lot of things that they've worked at for years and years and that just haven't come up to expectations. And they often live for long periods of time in quiet disappointment. Then something impels them into change. Good change or bad change. Or maybe no change at all, just capitulation to a dullness of life."

"Funny you should put it that way," he said. "My best friend dropped by my house last Sunday afternoon. He's been a leader in his church for twenty years, a major giver, with an outstanding reputation as a Christian. And you know what he said? He sat down and blurted out, 'I've just gone to my last church service.' I couldn't believe what I'd heard, and I asked him to repeat himself.

"He said it again, 'I've just gone to my last church service,' and then he explained. 'I was sitting there and realized that I'd been hearing the same stuff year after year. I'd been doing the same things. I'd been working on the same problems and not solving them. And I told myself that something wasn't working for me. Maybe it was for everyone else, but not for me. It wasn't making any difference. So I've decided that I'm not going back anymore.'"

I think there must be a lot of disappointed people in churches. They are disappointed in their lack of ability to be more faithful followers of Christ. They may or may not admit it, but they are disappointed in their church experience. But whom do you talk to about a vague feeling such as disappointment? They endure, hoping that somewhere along the line there will be a breakthrough of sorts.

A POSITIVE DISSATISFACTION

A third occasion that triggers dark-forest moments is a *positive dissatisfaction,* which I'll try to contrast with disappointment. We're talking of the person who awakens to the realization that he can actually do better. He can be deeper as a person; his mind can be more disciplined; his intersections with people can be of greater quality. His relationship with God can be more expansive. Unlike the second category, no one is being blamed. It is a quiet awareness that there is growing room, possibility for depth, breadth, or reach.

A working associate has carried forty extra pounds for years and not really worried about them. Suddenly, she engages in an effort of disciplined eating and exercise. The forty-eight-year-old wife of a close friend decides to return to school and start a master's program because she is concerned about quality in education. A man I know takes early retirement and volunteers to do a full-time job without salary at a cash-poor community agency. "Decided it was time to give back," he says.

These are all mid-course corrections of a kind that comes from a positive dissatisfaction and causes one to say, "I can do better."

Great athletes are never satisfied. Every Boston Celtics fan knew that Larry Bird shot hundreds of baskets in an empty arena hours before

17

every game. He knew he could do better. String musicians know that the late Pablo Casals played scales on his cello for four hours every day until the day he died in his mid-nineties. Admirers of Oliver Wendell Holmes know the story of President Roosevelt's visit to Holmes's home on the occasion of his ninety-second birthday. The president found him reading Plato and asked him why. Holmes replied, "To improve my mind, Mr. President, to improve my mind." The apostle Paul wrote in his oldest days (and I paraphrase), "I want to know Christ so intimately that I share His sufferings, His death, and His resurrection."

Each person is telling us that he is dissatisfied with the status quo and wants to grow. And growth is a form of mid-course correction.

Naturally, it is a bit difficult to mate this third occasion with the picture of a dark forest where one comes, unhappily, to one's senses. And I'm not going to try very hard. I want to present you with a symmetry of ideas. The dark forest is a useful picture of the moment we shall all face, perhaps on many occasions, when we know that correction or change of a sort is necessary. Whether we are pressed in that dark-forest moment by the disintegration of life's structure, the nagging disappointments of things that aren't going well, or the genuine urge to upgrade the quality of our lives, we, like Dante, have come to our senses. Life-change is imperative.

And so, if I need to say it again, that's what this book is about: mid-course correction—transformation, change, conversion. It's built on many of the things I've learned and come to appreciate since 1987. The book is called *Mid-Course Correction* because it is meant to speak to people who have done just enough living to recognize that life is tough and the answers are not easy.

The title is meant to imply lots of hope: that we can be new and different people at any time in life. Don't let anyone ever tell you that change is impossible. We are renewable people. I know. I've been in several dark forests. One actual. Several others like Dante's. And I found the straight path.

Chapter 2

Words That Convert

A sentence in a book review leaped off the page at me a few weeks ago. The writer was expressing delight in the work of a newly published poet. Of one particular poem he wrote, "It goes straight to the heart and thrives there."

The sentence caused me to think of times in my life when words went straight to the heart and thrived. To thrive meant that the words lingered and were not forgotten. It meant that they lodged in the heart and compelled attention and action. To thrive meant that the words became part of the things I wanted to communicate to people in my world.

Think of words and strings of words that we often hear and cease to believe. Therefore, they never reach the heart: "Your call will be answered in the order in which it was received"; "With this verse I'd like to conclude"; "I'll do it on Saturday"; and "You can fly to Hawaii and stay for seven days and nights, all for $99." None of these statements tend to, as they say, move us. We've heard them before, and we no longer believe them.

But some words and messages do move us. In fact, they change our lives. For reasons that we may not always understand, they reach us in force, drive into our deepest selves, and thrive there.

The words of my wife (at the time my fiancée), Gail, after she heard me make an attempt at preaching, went to my heart and thrived. We had been dating for only a month or two but were already falling in love. A pastor kindly invited me to give a talk at his church's midweek service. I was only twenty-three, but I did my best to prepare. When my talk was over and people had offered encouraging remarks, Gail and I slipped out into a back hall of the church. She threw her arms around me, kissed me, and gave me her opinion that God was going to make me into a preacher. I never forgot that embrace, the kiss, those words. They helped make me a preacher. We call such words an affirmation.

On the other hand, I recall the words of a close friend many years ago as we walked the sidewalks of a Japanese city. I had made a very unkind remark about someone we both knew. He stopped and looked at me squarely. "Gordon," he said, "a man who loves God would never say a thing like that about a brother."

The words went into my heart and thrived in an entirely different way. We call such words a rebuke. Tough words like these are designed to go to the heart and thrive. In this case the words thrived because I still hear them today. On any occasion when I feel the temptation to make a similarly unkind remark about anyone, I hear my friend from years ago say, "A man who loves God would never say a thing like that about a brother." I have been saved countless times from slandering someone because of this one sharp rebuke.

"Proclaim a gospel of the second chance," said a dear friend, who charged me to return to preaching twelve years ago when for almost two years my voice had been silent. With such a statement he set in motion a new vision of possibility, a ministry that had as its target those who think they are without hope of any sort of mid-course correction in life. We call such words a challenge. Like the affirmation and the rebuke, the challenge entered my heart and thrived there.

Think back and recall similar times in your journey when there was the perfect blend of people, circumstances, and heart-alertness. Words were spoken, and they engaged not only the mind and electrified not only the emotions but went to the heart and prospered.

What is the evidence that this has happened? We change.

A couple of years ago I had the privilege to be a speaker at a conference that also featured Dr. Kenneth Cooper, the father of the aerobic exercise movement. When this man, several years older than I am, stood to speak, I instantly came to attention. His topic was the care of the body through exercise, diet, and vitamins. We preachers would say that he was his own best sermon illustration. He stood straight, and it was quite clear that there was not an ounce of extra weight on him. When he spoke, his words came in torrents: facts, statistics, stories that illustrated his points. He exuded a passion for his subject that no one could miss. His conclusions and challenges were so powerful that you felt like a fool if you didn't resolve to do what he said. His message went to my heart and thrived there.

When Gail and I left the room, I said to her, "I'm a converted man."

"What do you mean?" she asked.

"He was absolutely right. I'm going home to do what he said in there."

And I did. In the following months I changed almost everything about my eating and my vitamin regimen. As for adequate exercise, I'm still working on that. But the point is that change happened. I did make a mid-course correction.

John Sculley's description of the conversation he had with Steve Jobs of Apple Computer one evening in New York has always aroused my imagination. Jobs had tried again and again to recruit Sculley away from Pepsi-Cola to come and run Apple. No amount of money seemed enough to persuade Sculley.

In desperation Jobs finally said to Sculley, "Do you want to spend your life making sugared water, or do you want to help us change the world?"

It was as if he had been hit by a stiff punch to the stomach, Sculley would later recall. An impulsive question of immense significance had bored its way to the interior of his life. It had to have gone to Sculley's heart and flourished because soon he was on his way westward to join Jobs and Apple Computer.

But none of these words—the affirmation, the rebuke, the challenge of Kenneth Cooper, the searching question asked by Steve Jobs—compare with the words of Jesus and their capacity to zing straight to the heart when He engaged with people. What He said and how He said it had an immense effect upon people of all walks of life. No one, having heard Him, could remain spiritually motionless for long. Either people moved closer to Him, or they moved farther away. Whatever the direction, there was always movement. Our Lord was not an entertainer. He was an agitator of the soul, provoking people to think mid-course correction in life.

If you acquaint yourself with the transactions that Jesus had with the people of His time, you might be impressed, as I have been, that there were four kinds of folk who needed the personal rearrangement of life He came to make happen. People of each kind came toward Him with a different agenda, and sooner or later, each left having been nudged one step further along into the next of the four categories. True, more than a few slipped backward. But keep your eye on those who moved forward. I often tell the people to whom I give talks that every one of us can be found somewhere among the four and ought always to be asking what it might take to move one step further along. The movement from one to the other is part of what I call *conversion of life*.

SPECTATORS

The first of the four categories of people, also the largest and the most common of the four, is what I've come to call *spectators*. These men and women hang out around the Lord for essentially selfish reasons. More than a few spectators showed up wherever He appeared because they heard that He was a healer. And physical problems were abundant in those days. So they pressed Him for attention.

Some smelled political and social possibilities; others were curious about the ideas Jesus expressed in novel ways; and still more liked the fact that no one seemed to go hungry around Him.

Many other spectators, however, were there because they were just plain spiritually empty and knew it. They were bereft of anything like vital optimism, felt exploited by organized religion, and were terribly confused about what was right. For them, what Jesus said (to use the words of an old gospel song) were "wonderful words of life."

In contrast to those who came with a spark of anticipation was a darker group of spectators who stood at a distance, watched and listened, probing for weaknesses that they might use to discredit Him. When they took Him through tricky questions and challenges designed to put Him on the spot, they failed miserably and usually went away mad.

Spectators tend to remain anonymous. They move as a mob, jump quickly to conclusions, and are easily stirred to strong emotion. Spectators listen for just so long, and then they walk. Only a few stay. They will not, if they can help it, be sucked into anything that demands something of them. For spectators it's largely "take" and not "give."

If spectators show any group enthusiasm, it is generally short-lived. They may seek to crown you today, but they can, just as easily, crucify you tomorrow. Their initial expectations are simple: feed them, flatter them, make them feel good. You'll be their darling. But disappoint them, and they can turn nasty very quickly.

No wonder it was said of Jesus when He looked out over a crowd of spectators, "[He] would not entrust himself to them, for he knew all men. He did not need man's testimony about man, for he knew what was in a man" (John 2:24–25).

Jesus' treatment of spectators was not necessarily harsh. "He had compassion on them" is a common description of His attitude toward them. Reflecting the prophet Ezekiel's excoriation of corrupt and uncaring kings, the Lord also became enraged when He saw the lack of justice and mercy given to the common people.

Nevertheless, Jesus did little to encourage spectators to stick around in crowd formation. Frequently, He seems to have downsized them by enlarging on what it cost to be servants of the real kingdom. The lightweights soon dispersed.

I think my first awareness of people as spectators came in my early years as a young pastor. I began a monthly breakfast for men, which jumped in attendance to (I'm guessing) two hundred. An ex-army cook prepared the food, and I gave a talk on issues pertinent to the lives of men. The mayor of the town began to attend, and with him came other members of the town government and business community. To me, it was all an indication that we had a revival under way.

But that was not to be. The mayor and his entourage (nice people that they were) were looking for votes for the upcoming election. After he was reelected, the size of our breakfasts was suddenly cut in half.

The Lord would have understood this. He fully appreciated the fact that words, no matter how wonderful, do not reach every heart or necessarily thrive there. But in those cases where spectators actually do hear and the words do thrive at soul-level, you have the possibility of men and women who take a step forward and become . . .

SEEKERS

Spectators dominated the landscape in a story related in John 6. A large crowd had gathered around Jesus "because they saw the miraculous signs he had performed on the sick." What's more they wouldn't go away. Over a period of two or three days, they followed Jesus everywhere. At one point Jesus fed them from the baskets of bread and fish, which He miraculously multiplied from a small boy's lunch.

"[You follow me]," Jesus finally said to them, "because you ate the loaves and had your fill. Do not work for food that spoils, but for food that endures to eternal life, which the Son of Man will give you."

This and other comments gained their attention, and He spoke, calling them to a deepening understanding of what life-change might entail. And that's when the spectators began to disappear: "On hearing it, many of his disciples said, 'This is a hard teaching. Who can accept it?' . . . From this time many of his disciples turned back and no longer followed him." Put simply, He tightened the screws of commitment, and the spectators bailed.

But some remained. And they were the emerging *seekers*. Characterize seekers as curious people. They ask questions, observe everything very carefully, take tentative steps forward to get closer to Jesus. What sets them in contrast to spectators is their awareness of a possible commitment to life-change. They know that mid-course correction is a distinct possibility, and they are saying to themselves, *I've got to learn everything I can; this could change me.*

A young man both of means and of power came to Jesus with a question about eternal life. The questions he asked were the questions of a seeker. And it is fair to suggest that the words of Jesus went to his heart, but did not thrive. When Jesus laid out the potential cost ("sell all you have and give it to the poor"), it was too much. We will never know what would have happened if he had begun to do what Jesus asked.

On the other hand, a woman by the name of Mary, sister of Martha, is said to have sat at His feet where she could take in every word He said. Given the cultural norms of her world, Mary's place was in the kitchen along with her sister, but she was too far along as a seeker. Her spiritual curiosity overcame the priority of so-called women's work.

The seeker is an earnest person and should be treated as such. He should not be pushed or shoved into a faster pace of spiritual awakening than he can thoughtfully handle. Jesus forced Himself on no one.

Andrew, who would later become a disciple of the Lord, was a seeker when he first appeared in the Gospels. Driven by curiosity, he and a companion kept tailing Jesus at a distance. When Jesus stopped and inquired about what they wanted, their question was, "Where are you staying?" To which Jesus responded, "Come and you will see."

This is the seeker in motion: following hard on the steps of Christ, learning everything possible to be learned. This is how real faith is forged, vital optimism generated. It is accomplished not in some highly charged atmosphere of persuasion but in quiet, reflective engagement with the Lord.

Andrew's experience speaks for itself. Before the day was out, Andrew was on his way to find his brother, Simon, to whom he said, "We have found the Messiah." And, the writer noted, "he brought him to Jesus" (John 1:35–42).

One never wants to disturb the musings of a seeker. It is possible for a person to remain in this category for a long period of time. He will watch; he will listen; he will ask questions; he will always be around. And what will finally cause the seeker to cross the line of faith and when it will happen are anyone's guess. But this one thing is sure: a mysterious Voice out of heaven will speak into the seeker with words that go to the heart and thrive there.

A man and his family begin worshiping with our congregation. When I introduce myself to him and invite him to lunch, he says, "I would enjoy meeting you, but I need to tell you one thing. I'm here only because my wife needs church. Personally, I have no need of it whatsoever. I really don't believe in God at all."

When we meet a few days later, he repeats this disclaimer once again. And I accept it with the comment, "Hey, if you feel you have to be there on Sunday, why not simply say at the beginning of each worship time, 'God, I don't think You're here, but if You are, let me hear Your Voice'?"

"I could do that," he says.

Months later I saw my friend at a weeknight event where a space engineer gave a talk about his own journey of faith. At the end of the evening, I noted that the two went off together. A day or two later I crossed paths with the speaker.

"I noticed you talking with John the other night. What did he say?"

"He said he was angry that I'd gotten into his life with my talk. Said I'd talked about Christ in a way that made perfect sense to him. So we went upstairs to the sanctuary and he asked Jesus to come into his life."

Words, wonderful words of life, had entered a heart and thrived there.

When I saw John the next Sunday, he was beaming. He was carrying a new Bible that his wife had given him as a symbol of his commitment. It had taken months, and my friend had not made a big deal of it. But he had crossed the line into faith in Jesus and was now among the . . .

FOLLOWERS

From among the *spectators-become-seekers,* there appear a few who become *followers.* This transition is the greatest of all mid-course corrections. It is that initial transformation, it is said, over which the angels of heaven rejoice.

Biblical people believe something very special happens when this line is crossed. The term that comes to mind is the acquisition of *saving faith.* A man or woman has been in a dark forest, and suddenly, a burst of light cuts through the gloom. There is a new sense of direction, an invigorating power to the heart.

In one of the most oft-quoted descriptions of how one becomes a follower of Christ, C. S. Lewis tells in *Surprised by Joy* how he came kicking and screaming into the kingdom:

> You must picture me alone in that room in Magdalen [Oxford], night after night, feeling, whenever my mind lifted even for a second from my word, the steady, unrelenting approach of Him *whom I so earnestly desired not to meet.* That which I greatly feared had at last come upon me. In the Trinity Term of 1929 I gave in, and admitted that God was God, and knelt and prayed: perhaps, that night, the most dejected and reluctant convert in all England. I did not then see what is not the most shining and obvious thing; the Divine humility which will accept a convert even on such terms. (Emphasis mine)

This mid-course correction of which Lewis speaks is at the center of the entire biblical story. From the earliest pages of the Scriptures we read about ancient people who defied God and adopted patterns of thought and action. Every generation since has emulated their choices, each in its own "creative" way. Yet the Bible also tells of a God who speaks into this moral and spiritual morass and calls out with words of love designed to go to the heart and thrive there. This is the Voice (with a capital *V*) that has never stopped speaking and inviting people to follow.

The early disciples about whom I will have much more to say later are our best models of seekers-become-followers. In ones and twos, they separated themselves from the seekers and acknowledged Christ's invitation to a journey. Their lives became thoroughly redirected. They learned to think differently, relate to strangers and to one another in new ways, and see their vocations from a fresh perspective.

Following had its bumps. As they came after Jesus, they had to come together and discovered that they didn't always like one another. As they learned to engage with people, they found that they didn't always like the people they were asked to serve. All the darknesses of the human spirit began to reveal themselves in these new followers. Someone with less character than Jesus would have fired them all and started over. But He hung with them, and you know the rest of the story.

I said there were four categories of people drawn toward Jesus. Which means that I do not think *following* is the end of the road. To become a follower of the Lord means to become so identified with Him in character that similarities begin to appear. The apostle Paul described it in these words: "I no longer live, but Christ lives in me" (see Gal. 2:20). The traditional word describing Paul's idea is *union* (as in "union with Christ"): a relationship perceived of as so tight that it is difficult to distinguish where One (Christ) picks up and the other (Paul) leaves off.

But I do think that one added step remains to be highlighted. A step that recognizes the mission or the purpose of Jesus. "Christianity is not designed to help you get your life together," Henri Nouwen once told a journalist. His comment was based on an impatience toward those who have attempted to reconfigure Jesus from Savior and Lord to a therapist whose task it is to make us feel good.

Perceptive followers will ultimately come to a moment when they discover that it is the purpose of Jesus through mid-course correction to make us into servants (not kings) to our generation in His name. In so doing we become . . .

KINGDOM-BUILDERS

Kingdom-builders are *followers* who have finally gotten the message that there is more to following than, well, just following. They come to the insight that their faith must radiate, in both humility and vital optimism, Christlike character, familylike commitment to a spiritual community, and servantlike activity in the world. Not everyone who calls himself a follower ever fully discerns this.

I confess an impatience with the Christian movement of evangelicals to which I belong when we call ourselves Christians with a breezy ease, as if we were the only ones entitled to this name. We take an astonishing liberty (when you think about it) to label others, Christians or non-Christians, on the mere evidences of a conversionist's formula. What it would be wise to seek, much superior to words, would be the evidences that kingdom-building is a way of life for a person. For this is authentic Christianity; this, I believe, is the true Christian: he who reflects Christ in the fullness and uniqueness of his mission. Words (all the words in the world) are not enough.

I call these qualities kingdom-building because they reflect the challenge a king once gave to his servants in a story Jesus told. He was going away, and he placed certain resources in their hands, telling them, "Make a profit with this until I return."

As one servant later found out, it was not enough to merely protect what he had been given. He was to become proactive. He was to "build" his master's kingdom through an investment of what had been entrusted to him.

I have had the privilege of knowing many would-be kingdombuilders over the years. Some started into this category of the spiritual journey with a vision and enthusiasm that were awesome to behold. And then, somewhere along the way, they lost it all. But many others have moved ahead in strength.

Almost thirty years ago I met Duncan Miller, a brilliant young manager in the fledgling computer industry. One day he informed me that he had a sense of call to get involved with a Bible study for prisoners. Charles Colson had not yet inflamed the Christian community with his call to prison ministry, so Duncan's vision was rather unique to us.

Duncan began to go behind the walls of Concord (Massachusetts)

Correctional Institution (CCI) every Monday night and teach the Bible. He has hardly missed a night since that inauspicious beginning. Over the years many have followed him, been trained by him, and extended his vision to all parts of the prison. Recently, he showed me a complete Bible study curriculum designed for men and women in the prison world that has been instrumental in introducing scores of inmates to faith in Jesus.

Today, Duncan Miller leads a high-level task force in the Defense Department that coordinates computer simulation programs for the training of our military. He is highly respected in his profession. But his vocation is prison work. He is a kingdom-builder.

I am drawn to kingdom-builders who quietly and consistently serve and resist the recognition that brings praise to them rather than the Lord they serve.

As I wrote earlier, I often refer to the four kinds of people who surrounded Jesus when I give talks to men or to crowds of people where I have not been before. I try to make the point that those of us (well, most of us) who are hungry for life-change could do no better than to place ourselves in one of the four categories and then decide where to go from there.

I hear myself saying, "Are you among the spectators who are always dabbling in this or that, wanting change *if* it fits one's convenience? Or do you find yourself a seeker, believing in the possibility of mid-course correction but concerned that it be done in a correct and timely manner? Perhaps you're a follower who is confident that you've declared yourself on Christ's side of the line, and you're working out the commitment to absorb His character. And where are the kingdom-builders: men and women who think 'vocation' and have become obedient to His call to the servant-life?"

Thus the question du jour: What will it take to make you move one step ahead in your life of faith? That will happen only when you hear the words of the Voice deep within that go to the heart and thrive there.

Chapter 3

GENUINE CHANGE

It was a Sunday night in a Baptist church, and I was the guest preacher. As in most Baptist churches, the people sang for at least a half hour. Since I am of Baptist roots, I knew all the songs and heartily joined in.

Then the program called for a quartet of young men from a local Bible college to sing. Impeccably dressed, all in similar clothing, they'd obviously been well schooled in how to look attentively and admiringly at whoever was speaking or singing a solo and how to project excitement about their faith and their mission of representing their school.

The quartet's tenor was the spokesman, and after identifying himself, he courteously introduced all the others. Then he launched into what we Baptists call a testimony.

A testimony is an account of how one has made what I believe is life's initial mid-course correction and comes to personal faith. Put together thoughtfully, it is usually a three-point story: a description of life in a dark forest before faith, a description of coming to the straight path of faith (when, how, and why), and, finally, a sense of what difference has occurred as a result.

From the vantage point of one who grew up in a church where narratives of spiritual transformation are highly significant, I can tell you that the best testimonies are those based on a graphic prefaith story. Before the days of television, testimonies were a kind of church entertainment, and one could hear some rather candid stuff about what life outside the orbit of the church could really be like. Usually, one's imagination had to be employed to tease out certain parts of many accounts because the storyteller was constrained to use a certain amount of discretion in telling the facts.

Duke University professor William Willimon describes a testimony by a woman who had no history in a church and obviously wasn't aware of the need for appropriate discretion. Speaking of a recent moment she believed evidenced the onset of a spiritual transformation in her life, she described how her boyfriend had tried to coerce her into robbing a 7-11 store with him. They had done things like this before, but now she was finished. Something was going to be different from this time forth:

> Something in me, it says, "No, I've held up [a] gas station with you, but I ain't going to hold up no convenience store." He beat the hell out of me, but I still said no. It felt great to say no, 'cause that's the only time in my life I ever said no to anything. Made me feel like I was somebody.

This is the core of a testimony with great possibilities.

As I survey the many testimonies I heard when I was young, the most stirring were from men who had done time in prison, had been involved in excessive drinking, or had gone through a dramatic battlefield experience.

Second in line were the stories of people who had been obscenely wealthy, had done everything, been everywhere, and had lost it all. But now that they "had Jesus," they were happier than they'd ever imagined possible. As I imagined the sports cars, the mansions, the trips around the world, and the season tickets of the first part of their testimony, I confess that their claim to a higher level of happiness in the third part often strained my credulity.

There were testimonies from highly successful businesspeople, champion athletes, and those who had come back from terrible injuries or sicknesses. They also told stories of amazing dark-forest moments that usually resulted in sudden and powerful life-change and a discovery of a new vital optimism about life.

The second part of the standard testimony usually had to do with the mid-course correction itself—how it happened, where, and when. The more dramatic this event, the better the testimony. Had it occurred at a Graham crusade, while an airplane was in the midst of an emergency landing, when one learned that a son or daughter was on drugs? What was said to God? How did one feel at that moment? We listeners wanted to know.

Charles Colson tells of the dark-forest moment when he had left the home of his friends Tom and Gert Phillips, with whom he had spent an evening at the height of the Watergate scandal. Colson's life was imploding, and Phillips had talked to him about a mid-course correction into faith. Colson had listened courteously, begged off, and then gone to his car.

Outside in the darkness, the iron grip I'd kept on my emotions began to relax. Tears welled up in my eyes as I groped in the darkness for the right key to start my car. Angrily, I brushed them away and started the engine. "What kind of weakness is this?" I said to nobody . . . Why hadn't I prayed when he gave me the chance? I wanted to so badly. Now I was alone, really alone.

Driving away from the Phillipses' home, he felt a compulsion to pull over and think some more.

With my face cupped in my hands, head leaning forward against the wheel, I forgot about machismo, about pretenses, about fears of being weak. And as I did, I began to experience a wonderful feeling of being released . . . And then I prayed my first real prayer. "God, I don't know how to find You, but I'm going to try! I'm not much the way I am now, but somehow I want to give myself to You." I didn't know how to say more, so I repeated over and over the words: *Take me.*

Take my word for it: By any standard I know, this is the beginning of one powerful testimony.

There is a third part of the standard testimony I've become used to hearing: what *difference* had been made. Frankly, the third portion was often predictable as people spoke of contentment they'd never known before, freedom from guilt, and a love and appreciation for church which, in my childhood, I could never fully appreciate. This kind of storytelling was and is a serious part of our tradition.

Today testimonies still live, and they are often featured on Christian television or put into book form. Sometimes there is a bothersome and glitzy sensationalism. All too often, it seems, twenty-seven-year-old (or something) people are encouraged to write their autobiographies and tell us a lot more than we need or ought to know.

When I was young, it was not difficult to become cavalier about testimonies because I had the feeling that some stories either were told too soon or were too old.

To tell one's story too soon was dangerous because it was not yet clear where the mid-course correction was leading, how deep into the heart it had really gone, and whether there were going to be some crashes along the way. Sometimes a testimony was too old: a story long in the past that had no continuing track record to show that it led to something of consistent spiritual substance.

A friend tells of the day long ago when, as a university student, he became utterly burned out on drugs and sexual promiscuity and found himself in a Christian community trying to put the broken pieces of life together. There he discovered the need for a mid-course correction into faith in Jesus. Soon after that he wisely sought spiritual direction in order to deepen his commitment. His search resulted in spiritual oversight of a nun who agreed to offer guidance but insisted, as a condition, that he submit all decisions regarding his new faith for her approval. He agreed.

A few months after this commitment, my friend was invited to give his testimony to a stadium full of young people. Doubtless, he could have told a stirring story. When he asked the permission of his spiritual director to accept the invitation, she said, "And what will you tell them?"

"I'll tell them my story," he responded.

Calling him by name, she said firmly, "You have no story . . . yet." Please stop and think about these words: "You have no story . . . yet."

Reflecting on that moment, my friend observed many years later, "It was true. I had no story that was worth telling yet. Not enough life-change had happened. Had I defied her opinion, I don't know where I'd be today."

What I hear being said is that until the third part of a testimony has a substantial track record, perhaps it is not a real testimony, and perhaps it does the storyteller a bit of damage to tell it too soon.

Occasionally, there were and are fictional embellishments or exaggerations, but nevertheless, most testimonies are real stories, and they echo the vast emptiness and suffering through which people are always passing. There is no doubt that many lives are transformed through faith in Jesus, and testimonies give us a chance to hear how it works.

There came a day, during my college years, when I wrote out my testimony for the first time. I remember how difficult it was to do because my story seemed so banal. My prefaith experiences included nothing particularly memorable for those seeking some sort of titillation. My moment of mid-course correction into faith was not framed in great emotion, certainly not the equal of Paul's on the road to Damascus, and my description of personal transformation was rather unimpressive. My college roommate had a much more marketable testimony I thought, and we once discussed an exchange of stories as we left to speak at some campus meetings. He would tell my story; I would tell his. And then we said, "Nah . . ."

Remembering that I have all of this experience with testimonies in my background, you can understand why, on that particular night in the Baptist church where I was to be the guest preacher, I came straight out of my pew when the young tenor (about, let's say twenty years old) who was captain of the visiting quartet began his story in this fashion:

> I was sinking deep, deep in sin [which is really a plagiarism of an old Baptist hymn]. I was drifting further and further away from God. There was no temptation I did not face, no kind of evil that I wasn't attracted to [sic]. I was rebellious, defiant, and destructive. And then, praise God, *at the age of four,* I came to Jesus, and He changed my life. (Emphasis mine)

Of all the testimonies I have ever heard, his was the most remarkable. The implications made it difficult for me to get my mind back to the sermon I was to preach as I conjured up mental pictures of the kind of sinner this young man must have managed to be at the age of four. What does a four-year-old's dark-forest moment look like? And I thought of his parents and the relief his *life-change* from such profligacy must have brought to them.

The people of my faith tradition have been highly influenced by several generations of evangelism in which preachers went out across the countryside and proclaimed the gospel of Jesus and called for people to make mid-course corrections and come to faith in Jesus. And do it now! People were expected to take all this in, make a decision for

Christ, and if possible, respond to an invitation to go forward to the front where they would be prayed for and perhaps counseled about what to do next. Many years of this kind of activity have had considerable effect upon the way we have come to believe people first encounter God and experience mid-course correction.

What was terribly troublesome and beyond understanding was when one of the stories seemed to slide into reverse. And sometimes this happened. Of course, it wasn't related to us in the form of, shall we say, a *reverse testimony*. More often than not, we would hear of such deconversions in quiet conversations or in prayer groups where the details were transmitted in the form of a prayer request. But *reverse testimonies* were not featured at banquets, in books, or on TV programs.

I wish this were not so. We who passionately believe in the possibility of life-change do not help ourselves when we are not more candid about the fact that many people (observed over time) simply do not seem to change even when they appear to have done all the things appropriate to crossing the line into faith. Why do some men and women claim powerful conversions in their lives only to revert to former styles of life? This happens more often than anyone would wish to admit.

The tales of two young men come to mind.

I played a facilitating role in the first and second parts of the first man's testimony. He was among the most lovable, the most sincere men I have ever met. He could not have been more attentive to everything I taught, and when it came to mentoring toward faith, he was all ears. Highly gifted, he did well in his career, and he had every reason to contemplate a bright future.

There were darknesses in his life that included a serious addiction to cocaine. On several occasions in response to the prayers of our spiritual community, he would appear to have broken with his captivity to drugs, and we would rejoice. At the time he was in love with an impressive woman, and I presided at their wedding ceremony. Those who had known him for the previous years of his life attended the wedding and lavished praise on the changes they'd seen in his life. We were all sure that we were witnessing a miracle in progress.

But something went terribly wrong. The struggle with cocaine and other drugs revived. The marriage, now including a child, buckled. One day he disappeared. A few days later we heard that he was dead. Those of us who loved him, who had invested ourselves in him, were devastated.

We who talk so confidently about life-change do not know enough about what happens in an experience like this. In a community where success stories are the *tour de force,* it is disquieting to face up to why some mid-course corrections go awry. Such spiritual catastrophes do not fit in easily with our optimistic theology, so we do not like to talk about them.

I think of a second young adult man (which to me means the thirties) who was regarded as an outstanding follower of Christ. He was loved for his sensitivity, his thoughtfulness, his commitment to the congregation. In any discussion where there was a need for someone to lead who had extraordinary spiritual stature, his was the first name to be named.

This man had been converted in his nineteenth or twentieth year. He had been in a rock band touring the country. One night in what could be called a dark-forest moment, he had wandered into a church, been moved by what he heard, and by the end of the evening, made a personal commitment to Jesus.

He left the band, settled in that community, and pursued a deepening knowledge about the Bible and the general Christian life. It wasn't long before all the people in the church were reveling in the story of his mid-course correction. As the months passed he fell in love with one of the young women in the church, and she returned the favor. You can imagine the excitement at the wedding; the people of the community felt as if they were seeing the fruitfulness of their church's life together. A life had been transformed and was moving ahead in great stability.

A few years later that man and his wife and their children moved to the East to pursue career opportunities. And it was to our congregation that they came and established themselves as leaders and valuable friends. They were welcomed and appreciated.

Then one day (about twelve years or so into this testimony) the unimaginable happened. Suddenly, without any warning, this no-longer-so-young man moved out of his home, away from his wife and children. He seemed to revert to a life reminiscent of the one he'd left behind that Sunday years before. It was not a matter of unfaithfulness, that someone else had drawn away his affections. Just a collapse of faith really.

No one was more stunned than I. I am no stranger to seeing people cool off in their Christian commitment, but somehow the seeming deconversion of this man to an old way of life challenged me more than anything I'd seen before. I never saw him again; he walked out of our world. And we were left to wonder what it had all meant.

Was this what happened back in New Testament days when Paul wrote of one of his apostolic teammates: "Demas has forsaken me, having loved this present world, and has departed for Thessalonica" (2 Tim. 4:10 NKJV)? Did Demas tire of his faith experience? Were the attractions of a woman, a job offer, the pressures of persecution too much for him? Was it possible that Demas's original commitment to Jesus was not really a deep, but a superficial, change of life? Could this happen to any of us? Does Demas's leaving suggest that he had never really come to stay? Did Paul have any anticipation that this could happen?

The disappearance of this wonderful young man from our congregation, more than anyone else, caused me to think about life-change in a way I'd never thought about it before. It wasn't that my old view of Christian life and commitment had changed. But it might be, I told myself, that we had not thought enough about what happens when someone embraces faith in Jesus. Maybe we had much more to learn.

Some of the biblical writers raised similar questions, using the word *apostasy* as their descriptor of what happens when people deliberately renounce faith or choose evil ways of life to such an extent that they must leave the church. Is it possible, the first generation of Christians asked, for a person to be truly converted and then to lose all that he had gained as he reverts to a life of nonfaith? The early church fathers sweated that one out and never reached full agreement.

Some said no. It's impossible for one to be booted out of the family of God once he is in. Some said yes. One can throw away what he has been given. And they tried to define the specific conditions under which this might happen. And some said anyone who "apostatizes" was never truly converted in the first place. Case closed. The biblical movement has argued these positions for almost two thousand years without ever reaching a convincing conclusion.

Today I rarely hear anyone debate these issues. Doubtless there is vigorous discussion somewhere on the seminary campuses of our country, but the question gets little attention among the laity. Perhaps because most people find the old debate to be rather brittle and unhelpful.

One of the challengers for his party's nomination in the 2000 presidential election speaks of a fundamentalist Christian conversion during his college days. At the time, a small leaflet (or tract) told his story and quoted him as making a declaration of total "surrender" to Christ. At my age of sixty I'm not sure any twenty-year-old can conceivably understand anything about total surrender, but that's just an opinion.

Today, this aspirant to the presidency speaks of leaving that college-years conversion behind. Today, he says, he embraces many faiths and philosophies. Frankly, that sounds nice, crowd pleasing, and very postmodern.

His story of embracing and then unembracing Christian faith provides a challenge to my thought about deep Christian change. What happened to this man? Was his original conversion a sham, ingenuine? Was he lying back then? I don't think so.

But does he, on the other hand, live presently in what some would call a state of apostasy? A sort of rebellious or suspended faith? Rather than reduce his experience to an unsatisfying rationalization, and rather than sit in pretentious judgment, I would prefer to think quietly and humbly over these things and realize that we do great harm to the mystery of conversion when we reduce it to a convenient formula. And then watch our doctrine sag when someone presents us with a situation, like this one, that is so difficult to figure out.

Perhaps we have inadvertently limited the Bible's opportunity to speak to us on this matter. Maybe we need to go to other portions of Holy Scripture to gain a better balance on what mid-course correction means in the eyes of God.

Modern Christians (Christ-followers and kingdom-builders) have tended to look at the issue of transformation into faith only from a New Testament perspective. Would we profit from an Older Testament perspective? I think so. And that's why the following chapters head in that direction.

I have thought often, with a smile, of the night a twenty-year-old young man gave his testimony in such vivid detail. He is at least forty-five years of age now. I wonder if his story has changed.

Chapter 4

SELF-IMPROVEMENT OR TRANSFORMATION?

A sentence from a modern novel piques my interest. Referring to a man and a woman in their mid-fifties who, in their youth, had been part of the so-called hippie generation and had spent their days marching, burning draft cards and bras, and doing Woodstock, the narrator said, "Years ago I learned their dirtiest, most crabbed secret, that their passion to change the world derived from the fact *that they could not change themselves.*"

Like most everyone else, biblical people love self-improvement. Go to the typical religious bookstore, and see the thousands of titles that make incredible promises. We, like others, attempt to break habits, acquire disciplines, renounce things not beneficial, make vows to begin doing things that are. There is a lot about ourselves that we manage to change through the brute force of determination.

We lose weight, climb out of debt, stop biting our fingernails, give up smoking, repair a bad marriage, change work habits, and (this was one of mine) resolve to get oil changes in our cars every three thousand miles.

Self-improvement is nice. But I hope to write about transformation, deep change. Soul deep! Changes not implemented by ordinary means. These life issues are found deep in the interiority of our lives, far deeper in a sense than the floor of an ocean.

When I think of such change or mid-course correction, I think of our essential human nature passed down from our first father and mother in creation. Or the process by which we think and make judgments: a process formed and bred into us by scores of preceding generations in our gene pool. On a priority basis, I think the Bible would suggest the greatest unchangeable is our lost connection with God the Creator. In all these areas we are left with faint echoes of what might have been if evil, like a virus, had not invaded human life and left us out of touch with our deeper selves.

The prophet Jeremiah sensed this mysterious loss of connection when he spoke of the human heart:

> The heart is deceitful above all things and beyond cure.
> Who can understand it? (Jer. 17:9)

The novelist in the opening paragraph offers a perspective worth much reflection when he identifies a trait that most of us share. If you can't change something about yourself, try changing everyone else around you. Was that what some of the sixties were about?

It is not difficult for biblical people to rally around ambitious slogans such as "Let's change the world." But we must dream such dreams with greater humility. As the novelist suggests with his thoughtful comment, many would-be world-changers may actually be admitting that they feel impotent to do the first business: that of changing the heart.

The rest of this book speaks to the issue of what change looks like and how it might happen in the deeper parts of life. The baseline point is very simple: *the quality of change at life's center will influence change at the surface.* Do spiritual business at soul-level, and personality and relational issues will begin to come along for the ride.

But the fact is, and I will say this in a number of ways, most of us prefer to do our business at the surface. We invest the preponderant amount of our energies *out there* where we can see what is going on, where mystery is cut to the minimum, where people will take notice and reward us.

My world has been the church. And I have seen this instinct work on the surface all of my life. As a community, we would much rather build buildings, launch programs, create systems and structures to do the good works of change. On a personal basis, we would prefer to be boisterous and boastful, busy and burned-out than to enter the great inner space where the Father initially seeks our communion. Why we would prefer the former to the latter (and almost all of us, beginning with me, do) is a mystery to me. But we do.

The word *hidden* is about to repeatedly pop up on these pages. It will refer obviously to things not seen, not appreciated, and not easily understood. Please get used to it. But it is in encountering the *hidden* things that we are likely to discover the most satisfying and the most enduring mid-course corrections in life.

The first of the hidden things are the purposes of God. When we speak of God's purposes, we try to discern what in the world God might be up to. Not all of God's purposes are hidden or remain so. But realities and intentions known only to heaven await a revelation in order for us to understand.

"I have much more to say to you, more than you can now bear," Jesus told His disciples. "But when he, the Spirit of truth, comes, he will guide you into all truth" (John 16:12–13). Put simply, the disciples weren't prepared to make sense out of a lot of things happening to them. They were going to have to step out into the currents of life and trust that God would care for them.

When I was a small boy with an overactive, inquiring mind, I asked many questions of my father. Some he answered; others he dodged with the comment, "Someday I'll tell you about that."

I heard my dad refer to "someday" so many times that I imagined a magic day far off in the future when he would sit down and answer all those questions one after the other. I anticipated a quantum leap of knowledge about everything from sex to the amount of his income *to the disappearance of a certain person.*

Although that someday with my dad never came in the way I anticipated, there is a someday in the plan of God when full disclosure will be made. A day when many of His actions and intentions will be thoroughly unfolded for us. But in the meantime, we have to make a big decision. Will we trust the God of hidden purposes and believe that He knows exactly what He is doing even when events make absolutely no sense to us at all?

I do not need to make a list of all the things that throw many of us off course because we find such trust difficult. Earlier this week a colleague told me that a member of his staff had just quit. "Why?" I asked.

"She's had it with God," he said. "There have been some issues in her life that will not resolve. She holds God responsible."

Implication: God, she thinks, owes instantly and perfectly comprehensible explanations on demand.

On occasion I've been tempted in such a direction. But slowly, I've come to appreciate the possibility that a large part of what I don't know is tightly wrapped up in purposes that only God understands and that will be revealed some day.

Few people had to come to grips with the hidden purposes of God more than Abraham. Paul called him "the father of all who believe" (Rom. 4:11). I have come to revere him as one of the greatest men of all time. The changes in his life, beginning in the deepest parts, are absolutely mind-boggling to me.

When I was a boy, the radio provided an enormous amount of imaginative entertainment. At the top of my personal list of programs was *The Lone Ranger*, which came on at 7:30 P.M. (EST anyway) every

Monday, Wednesday, and Friday. Each night the "resourceful masked rider of the plains and his faithful Indian companion, Tonto," were introduced with the same words: "Nowhere in the pages of yesteryear can one find a greater champion of justice. Return again with us to those thrilling days when out of the past come the thundering hoof-beats of the great horse, Silver. *The Lone Ranger rides again.*"

Forgive my descent into childhood if I dote on those words that never ceased to thrill me. And their effect remains whenever I hear tapes of the old broadcasts.

Somehow I feel a similar exhilaration each time I reopen the Scriptures and return to a more ancient time when out of the past comes this dear father of all who believe, this remarkable man, Abraham. Believe me, I am not wasting your time to walk you through his story. As the cereal commercial cleverly put it, "Taste [him] again for the first time." Just watching the man learn, grow, reach maturity is a lesson in itself.

Please join me in getting to know him as he deals with the first of the great mid-course corrections: living in harmony with the hidden purposes of God.

The novelist writes, "Years ago I learned their dirtiest, most crabbed secret, that their passion to change the world derived from the fact that they could not change themselves."

Abraham could not change himself, but God could.

Life's Mid-Course Corrections
Begin with a Call to Leave Something

The LORD had said to Abram, "Leave your country, your people and your father's household and go to the land I will show you. I will make you into a great nation and I will bless you."

—GENESIS 12:1–2

From this time many of [Jesus'] disciples turned back and no longer followed him. "You do not want to leave too, do you?" Jesus asked the Twelve. Simon Peter answered him, "Lord, to whom shall we go? You have the words of eternal life."

—JOHN 6:66–68

Chapter 5

ON THE TRAIL OF THE TWINE

You know those massive, airport-sized hardware stores, the ones with inventories that range from microscrews to construct-it-yourself skyscrapers? I was at one recently looking for an inexpensive storage cabinet.

The good news was that I found what I wanted. But the bad news, and I should have anticipated this, was that what I wanted didn't fit into the rear of our Outback station wagon. Then I remembered that the Outback had a roof rack and realized that the cabinet could easily fit up there. That was a great idea except that I'd need something, rope or bungees, to tie the cabinet down, and I had none with me.

"Actually, that's not a problem," the salesperson (I mean the aisle vice president) said. "We have plenty of twine for customers up at the front door."

Just as he said, there it was, twine, lots of it, easily drawn off of an enormous roll. There was even a cutter, chained to the floor, making it convenient for anyone to lop off what he needed. With my new cabinet scanned and paid for, I measured out and cut four lengths of twine and headed out the door, pushing my newly purchased cabinet on a flatbed cart.

Finding the Outback in the parking lot was complicated by the fact that I'd forgotten where I'd parked, not an uncommon occurrence for a dreamer like me. I had to stop and ask myself, "Was it near the Mickey Mouse light pole or the Donald Duck pole?" "How," I thought out loud, "is a grown-up supposed to remember that?"

The search for the car made for a rather circuitous walk. But I finally found it and got set to lift the cabinet up and onto the roof rack.

That's when I saw it. A long trail of twine, stretching out in the direction that I'd just walked. Apparently, when I'd cut my pieces of twine from the roll at the store, I hadn't noticed that the end of the cord coming off the roll had gotten entangled with one of the cart's wheels. Ninety, perhaps one hundred yards of twine had peeled out behind me like the trail of bread crumbs in the old fairy tale. And along this trail of twine there were people (thousands of them, so it seemed to this ultrasensitive person) who had paused to watch me make a fool of myself. No one said a word. This is New England, you understand.

The only thing I could do was to rewind the twine, all several hundred feet of it. I followed the path I'd created past both the Mickey Mouse and the Donald Duck poles and all the other twists and turns I'd made in searching for the car. Approaching the store, I found two of the aisle vice presidents contemplating their strangely diminished role of twine and wondering where it had all gone.

Returning to the Outback, I thought about the trail of twine that had marked every step I'd taken. Strung out around one pole and then another, it had represented a simple and quite visible map of just a few exasperating moments in my life.

But what if such a twinelike map existed for the whole of one's life? What if we could retrace the footsteps of the years and examine all the critical thoughts and choices that had brought us to where we are? What might we learn? My bet is that we would get an extensive education on mid-course corrections: good ones and not-so-good ones.

The story of Abraham in the Older Testament reads like a trail of twine. It starts in a mysterious land about which the Bible has almost nothing to say and moves on to a wild, climactic moment on the top of a mountain in a region called Moriah in the land of Canaan. Go there to that mountain first! Start at the end of the twine and see what a champion of transforming faith in his peak moment really looks like. Only then shall we return to the beginning and see how it all got started.

Most of us know why Abraham is on the top of that mountain. It's one of the most notorious moments in all of biblical history. A stunning, bizarre moment that we can hardly take in all at once, especially if we are parents or grandparents and love our children more than life itself.

Of course, Abraham is not alone. His son, his only son, Isaac, is with him and has been bound up in a ritual manner reminiscent of ancient pagan ceremonial rites, laid upon an altar, and prepared for sacrificial death. When we reach the mountain's summit, Abraham is about to use a knife to take his son's life in response to the command of the Voice of God.

If we choose to stand off to one side and merely observe events with no sense of a larger story, we will doubtlessly be quite confused; perhaps a better word would be *repelled*.

We might ask, does Sarah, Abraham's wife and Isaac's mother, know anything about this? We might even ask, does *the* God we know as *the God of the Bible* know anything about this? On the surface of things, what we have is a horrific picture of a man preparing his son for a ritual sacrifice similar to the one carried out with some regularity by Canaanites, the locals, and by the people of Ur from which Abraham had originally migrated. Certainly, we think, no god that we have ever known would initiate this spectacle.

Frankly (and I am by no means the first to say this), everything in the civilized part of me wants to protest on Abraham's behalf, to ask, what kind of God would ask this of a man, and what kind of man would choose to obey?

But then again, one hundred years led up to this moment, one hundred years I've not experienced, one hundred years in which this man, Abraham, began to hear a Voice with a word that entered deep into his heart and thrived there. Perhaps they have come to share a communion I do not understand. Perhaps *hidden purposes* are going on that are not easily disclosed to the untrained eye. So I might be prudent to remain quiet and watch.

Those in touch with the story know, first of all, that the knife was never used on the son anyway. Just as Abraham moved into action, the Voice from heaven ordered him to stop, calling him by his name, "Abraham, Abraham!" When the Voice continued, it said in part, "*Now* I know that you fear God, because you have not withheld from me your son, your only son" (Gen. 22:11–12 emphasis mine). *Now!* As if this were a thing not fully ascertained—that Abraham feared God—before this moment. *Now I know!*

It took one hundred years to reach this *Now I know!* Say the phrase three times over but emphasize a different word in the sentence each time. "*Now* I know." "Now *I* know." "Now I *know*." Which emphasis did Abraham hear?

Not a lot of this makes sense without the trail of the twine. What you will find is a story of Abraham's *conversion* (not really an Older Testament word or concept), his own mid-course correction that took him from spectator to seeker: *the one who leaves.*

Circle back to earlier in the week and grasp the immediate background of the story. What had compelled Abraham to go up that mountain on that day? The answer is offered in some detail (Gen. 22).

Days earlier, Abraham had heard the voice calling out to him: "Take your son, your only son . . . and go to the region of Moriah. Sacrifice him there as a burnt offering."

"Early the next morning," we are told, "Abraham got up and saddled his donkey" and was on his way. No delay, no defiance, no bargaining. The man simply went! We might be tempted to say "too simply, too easily," except that we need to understand that Abraham had been listening to this Voice for many years and had determined ever so painfully that it was entirely reliable. As difficult as the command was, the man had reached a point in his life where he simply obeyed.

"When he said 'sit down,'" a football player said of famed football coach Vincent Lombardi, "we didn't bother to look for a chair." This appears to be the pattern of response in Abraham's life that morning. It had not always been that way, however.

The opening words of the story say that all of this was done to test Abraham. Test what? His ability to obey, to trust, to accept the fact that all things were God's. This mountaintop moment seems to be the final step in Abraham's lifelong mid-course correction, the final proving ground that will qualify him to be the father of all who believe.

As I watch Abraham move toward the mountain with his only son, a load of sticks, and *no lamb*, I say to myself, *If you dare compare Abraham's conversion with that of anyone else in the Bible, it won't really be a contest. Match his experience with the conversion of Saul of Tarsus, for example.*

The facts are clear: the man had much further to go in his experience of life-change. Saul of Tarsus already knew who Israel's God was; Abraham did not. Saul knew his Scriptures back and forth; Abraham had nothing but a Voice. Saul was, by virtue of his upbringing, a man whose essential character and morality were in alignment with biblical standards; Abraham's perspective was rooted in pagan customs. Saul merely had to reorganize his faith to understand the preeminence of Christ as Messiah, and he was on his way; Abraham had to experience a magnificent mid-course correction from head to toe, from soul to mind to emotions.

Three things about Abraham's faith show brilliantly in the days surrounding the incident on the mountain.

First, *there is a subtle evidence that Abraham has learned how to obey the Voice:*

Some time later God tested Abraham. He said to him, "Abraham!" "Here I am," he replied. Then God said, "Take your son, your only son, Isaac, whom you love, and go to the region of Moriah. Sacrifice him there as a burnt offering on one of the mountains I will tell you about." (Gen. 22:1–2)

The "here I am" is the first tip-off. Abraham has acquired listening skills over a period of time. He has learned to discern God's Voice, and he has learned the appropriate response. Sometimes the acquisition of those skills takes time.

"You're looking at me, but you're not listening to me," I can hear my father say to me as a boy. In school the teacher would write on my report cards, "He doesn't listen; he's somewhere else." Hard to cope with a future dreamer. But they were right. I had to learn to listen. So did a host of others. I'm in good company.

Moses, filled with a young man's ambition to leadership, kills an Egyptian soldier, thinking it a worthy thing. But it isn't. Result: he spends forty years in the desert learning how to listen to God before he moves back into action. A strange man, Balaam, is a poor listener and has to be taken down by a talking donkey before he awakens to the Voice of God. Eli has to train Samuel, the future prophet, how to listen and respond to the Voice before anything else. Jonah will not listen and gets into a heap of trouble. It is in listening that Mary, mother of our Lord, learns of her exalted role in the redemption story.

So Abraham is a listener, and the "here I am" demonstrates it. Furthermore, he obeys without delay. This, as we shall see, was not always Abraham's strong side. The man we see who "early the next morning . . . got up and saddled his donkey" is a much different man from the one in the earlier days when he first began his journey. He has come from a land where they connive and stall and yell a lot if they don't like what they hear. And that's the sort of man Abraham once was. The fact that he obeys early the next morning in this instance is no small matter. The man has come a long way. He is forever changed.

> When he had cut enough wood for the burnt offering, he set out for the place God had told him about. On the third day Abraham looked up and saw the place in the distance. He said to his servants, "Stay here with the donkey while I and the boy go over there." (Gen. 22:3–5)

"He set out for the place God had told him about." We will see shortly that this is little more than a reflection of an earlier time when God had told Abraham to go to a place that He would tell him about. There is obedience in this situation. Blind obedience? Not quite! An obedience of a deeper sort that has been molded over the years as Abraham has learned to trust in the *hidden purposes of his God,* purposes not always disclosed to others, perhaps at the time not even disclosed to Abraham. Nevertheless, Abraham has learned not to question but to obey.

The man who goes up this mountain has also learned to trust.

> ISAAC: Father . . . the fire and wood are here, but where is the lamb?
> ABRAHAM: God himself will provide the lamb . . . my son.

"The two of them went on together" (Gen. 22:6). The son trusts the father. The father trusts the Father.

You and I know that such trust was not built in a day. Was Abraham lying when he said what he said? Was he blowing Isaac off, as they say? Or did he really mean what he said? While I know some who choose the former explanation, I choose the latter.

There had been other times when Abraham would have instinctively doubted the Voice. A God who keeps His promises? No one heard of such gods in Abraham's former homeland. Anyone who would have believed a god back where Abraham had come from would have been considered a fool. Rather than believe, people spent their lives buying gods off, placating them, or worst case, capitulating to them. But trust them? No way!

Something deep and transforming has happened in these last one hundred years of life. Abraham has reached a point of complete trust. In earlier days he might have laughed sarcastically in such a moment. But now he is serious. God *will* provide. There had been a promise, and it had been reiterated several times. Abraham would have a son, and through him, a progeny equal in number to the stars in the desert sky would call the patriarch blessed. This is trust.

When Gail and I moved to New England in 1972, we were a young couple with two small children, ages five and eight. We had felt God's call to a wonderful congregation in Lexington, Massachusetts. But we also had serious misgivings. It was the heyday of what has been called the sixties. The universities of New England were generally in a wild uproar of protests against all things: some reasonable, some not so reasonable. Lexington in particular seemed a place of a radical kind of liberalism that was not friendly, so we thought, to our faith. What, we asked, would our children face in school? Would we lose them in this move as they were absorbed into this greatly changing culture? We waited and wondered.

Two days after we arrived, the phone rang. The man at the other end of the line identified himself as the principal of the school where our children would attend. Would our children like to visit the school before the fall term began? he asked. They could tour the school, be registered, get to know him.

The next afternoon I took our two rather apprehensive children to Fiske School. As he had promised, the principal was at the front door to greet them. I watched as he tenderly escorted our son and daughter to their future classrooms, showed them pictures of their teachers, ushered them to the rest rooms, to the library, to the gym, to the lunchroom. The way he treated them, the way he spoke, caused me finally to say, "You're a follower of the Lord, aren't you?"

"Yes, I am," he said. "And I knew you'd be a bit nervous about what your children were getting into here in Lexington. I wanted to put your mind at ease. They'll be in good hands."

I learned that day to *trust* the God who had called us to New England, often said to be the graveyard of preachers. For us it became ground to thrive on. God was there; He'd called us there; and we'd learned to trust Him.

Come back to the mountaintop one more time, this place at the end of Abraham's trail of twine. A son lies on what we presume is an altar. He is bound and prepared for ritual death. In younger years Abraham had most likely seen similar scenes in his birth land. There, sons had been carried to the top of ziggurats (pagan temple sites), sometimes used in rites presumably saturated with sexual events, and then sacrificed to the gods. He'd seen these things; he knew what to do.

Must I say it again? I hate this moment in the story. With my eye I see all that I think I need to see: a father is about to *kill* (there is no other appropriate word) his child. Why would he be willing to do this?

Because (and this is the third mark of Abraham's faith) *Isaac is not his.* The child is God's, just as everything else is in Abraham's life. This son for whom he had longed all of his adult life, this son who he assumed would be the conveyer of his seed, the doorway to his progeny, is not his. This son is God's.

How long did Abraham have to live to learn this?

In the past the people of my faith tradition would often stand in church and sing,

> Take my life and let it be
> Consecrated, Lord, to Thee . . .
> Take my silver and my gold,
> Not a mite would I withhold.

We don't sing this song much anymore. Perhaps because we have a lot more silver and gold now than in the days when the hymn was written. Now, the song may meddle too much in our personal affairs.

As unthinkable as Abraham's intention in sacrificing his son was, we must take one more look at the moment in the context of his culture. He had come from a world where men did this sort of thing as part of their routine religious experience. There is a sense in which we have to ask whether Abraham could ever have demonstrated his trust and obedience for his God if he had not been willing to go as far as other men did in the worship of their gods.

Our modern minds recoil at this thing Abraham seems willing to do. We wonder what it will do to Isaac even if he isn't murdered. We ask what Sarah, Abraham's wife, will do. Perhaps we even ask if Abraham is capable of maintaining his sanity after this moment ends, however it ends.

But the fact is that Abraham is prepared to give back to God what he knows is not his in the first place. And if God asks for his only son, then he is prepared to go the distance.

But he doesn't have to.

"Stop, Abraham. Now I know that you fear God."

The frightful moment is over. And there will not be another one quite like it until God's only Son, Jesus, undergoes an experience similar to this one. Only in that case, the "knife" will not be restrained.

The trail of Abraham's twine is years and years long. We have only now seen the last inches. If we are to understand the nature of mid-course correction at the deepest level, we must go backward along the trail of the twine and see what made this man what he became.

And it's worth the effort. For anyone in search of life-change, Abraham's story from beginning to end is an absolute must.

I believe the transformation of Abraham will be the premier model of faith for the twenty-first century in the Christian community, a more helpful model than that of any other biblical person.

Chapter 6

LIKE AN OLD CHILDHOOD GAME

"Gordon, you may take three giant steps *forward.*"
"Mother, may I?"
"Yes, you may."
"Gordon, you may take two baby steps forward."
"Mother, may I?"
"No, you may not; take four giant steps *backward.*"

It was a childhood game. For lack of a better name, we called it Mother-may-I. I think girls loved it more than boys did because the game was a gender-leveler. A girl, playing the role of "mother," could give other girls an advantage over the boys just by the way she permitted people to advance *or* forced them to retreat a step or two. If "mother" was the vindictive sort, you could spend more time going backward than forward.

I see Abraham's life as similar to a game of Mother-may-I. Walking the trail of his twine, I visualize a man moving ahead, then losing ground, then moving ahead again. *In this, I think his life resembles mine!*

We started at the end of the twine of Abraham's story. Now join me at the beginning, at least as far to the front of his life as we can get. It really is worth going back now to the trailhead, where the life-journey of this man began.

If you trace Abraham's steps backward—from end to beginning—the trail will wind down that awful mountain where we just were and across the plain. It will twist and turn all over Canaan and then spike as far south as Egypt and back again to the north and finally eastward down the Fertile Crescent to the man's birthplace, the city of Ur. It is a good trip to take; you'll see yourself in surprising ways (as I have seen myself). All along the trail you will pick up the ideas that shaped this man's understanding that God was not merely a source of occasional luck but a sovereign, personal God with purpose and promise. Purposes often hidden, promises sometimes afar off. It was no easy process; Abraham was put through the wringer. But that's the price to be paid for anyone who would one day be called "father of all who believe."

The trail is marked with places where Abram (his earlier name meaning "exalted one") made a perfect fool of himself, places where he displayed hints of emerging nobility. Always learning, always growing, Abram's personal transformation was obviously a long, slow process—much more characteristic of the mid-course corrections most of us face—no overnight changes in his world or in most of ours.

ABRAM'S BIRTHPLACE

Abram's birthplace was Ur, part of the confederation of cities in Mesopotamia generally known as Sumer. Today we know that region as Iraq. He is assumed to have descended from the ancient wandering tribe of Semites (Aramaeans) who had finally settled down to city-building a few centuries back.

We learn nothing of Abram's earliest life from the biblical literature. What we are able to surmise comes from the work of historians and archaeologists who give us a rather detailed picture of civilization in that land.

It's apparent that the culture of Abram's homeland was advanced. Business, trading, and agriculture characterized the life of his people. A vigorous pagan religious perspective proliferated and shaped the way people thought. It is not surprising then that the tallest and most prominent structure in the community would have been the temple where rites were conducted that included sacred prostitution, human sacrifice, and a serious inquiry into the messages of the stars and planets of the heavens.

The Abram who enters the pages of the Bible in early Genesis comes out of a world where life was thought to be in the vise grip of fate. People lived with a sense that nothing ever changed. This is worth repeating: In the world of Abram's birth, *nothing purposely changes.*

If nothing changes, then there is no such thing as hope, no such thing as the pursuit of personal growth, no such thing as the expectation that tomorrow might offer more than today. To aspire to learn more than your fathers knew or to do things differently from the way your father did them would have been a serious blasphemy. Living in Abram's world meant taking your place in the parade of the generations, aspiring to nothing but a repetition of life as your fathers had known it.

It will be difficult for moderns to understand this, but the ancients did not possess a reflective, inner life. We who look within and analyze our own actions, literally talk to ourselves, build imaginative castles in the air, would not fit into Abram's world. In his time, one took one's life cues from the traditions and the shared experiences of the family-clan and the community. Life offered relatively few choices, little freedom.

We, who are the inheritors of a culture that worships at the shrine of progress, cannot even begin to imagine a world like this. No inspirations, no sense of a future, nothing to dream about.

As Thomas Cahill and others have pointed out, Abram's people saw all of reality like a wheel, slowly turning, always coming back to where it started. In such a world beginnings and endings were meaningless. Even the folk stories of the day, Cahill says, seemed to begin in the middle and stay there. It didn't occur to people to ask where things came from or where they were going. Life just was, as people found it.

This is the moment to go back to the beginning of this book and recover a term I used on the very first page: *vital optimism,* hope. In Abram's world there was none! There was no hope.

In Abram's world there was an abundance of gods. But they were gods who did not speak because they did not care. If the people wanted to beg, placate, appease the gods, that was their business. No one seriously expected the gods to deal fairly or justly in return. Religion was, more or less, a crapshoot of efforts to claw a bit of sense out of the mysterious.

The significance of going back this far into Abram's world lies in the fact that this is a book about mid-course corrections, *life-change.* In Abram's background, such a thought was inoperative; *it didn't exist.* Again, because the point is indispensable to where we're going in this book, people did not change, nor could they imagine change.

Personal change is generally a matter of individual choice. But individual choice did not exist in such a culture. One did what the community did; one thought what the community thought. To engage Abram or anyone in his world and suggest something like a biblical conversion, a transformation of life, would have been absurd.

Thus, we are reading about a showstopper when we go back to the beginning of Abram's trail and learn that somewhere along the way he heard a Voice (a sound from heaven that went to his soul and thrived there) saying, *"Leave!"*

"The LORD had said to Abram, 'Leave your country, your people and your father's household and go to the land I will show you'" (Gen. 12:1). It is virtually the very first thing we hear of Abram in the Genesis writing: "The LORD had said to Abram, 'Leave.'"

In Abram's world, no one ever left! No one thought of leaving. No one dared to leave. Perhaps society occasionally ostracized or shunned an errant person and exiled him from community life (which would have amounted to execution). But leaving out of one's free will? No way!

If the Voice had ever called out to anyone else in Sumer to leave, we don't know about it. Perhaps the only people with any sort of knowledge of life beyond the horizon were traders, and they always came back.

In a delightful movie called *A League of Their Own*, Tom Hanks plays a baseball manager who is hired to coach a professional team of women. When he speaks harshly to one of the players, she begins to cry. Hanks is astonished. In all of his days of coaching, he has never seen this happen before. Suddenly, he blurts out, "Listen to me. You don't cry in baseball. Do you hear me? You don't cry in baseball." His words are not that helpful to the distressed player.

In Abram's world you don't say *Leave!* I can almost hear Abram saying something to that effect as the Voice bores in on him: "Listen to me. You don't say *Leave!* in Ur."

But the Voice speaks anyway: "Leave!"

Leave what? "Your country, your people and your father's household [or clan]." Underlying this command to leave is a sense of totality. Abram is to leave everything that is familiar, safe, meaningful. *And he will not be able to return.* This is not a summer cruise.

A scholar of ancient languages points out the command that Abram heard, "Leave!" is encased in a verbal form that can be appreciated only as loud and forceful in character. It is a word spoken with brute force, crashing its way into the heart of this man. It bursts through the cultural barriers hardened by the centuries.

How powerful was the Voice that called this man? Perhaps, in a proverbial sense, this Voice is comparable to the power of the rocket thrusters pushing the space shuttle away from the gravitational force of the earth. We moderns who come and go, move from place to place in the world, change relationships at whim, have no idea what it meant for Abram to defy the gravitational force of his culture. The command to *leave* spoken by the Voice had to break the power of a thousand cultural *stays*.

The command to leave is accentuated by the reiteration of three things. Leave your *country*. Most ancient people rarely traveled more than a few miles from their birthplace in an entire lifetime. The world beyond the horizon was too scary. There were no maps, no route signs, no points of familiarity (McDonald's, Marriott, and Mobil Oil). Linguistic dialects would change from town to town. Leaving one's base of familiarity was an unthinkable thing to do.

Leave your *people*. Because one did not have a private world within one's personal life where individual decisions and judgments were made, one could not afford to be away from his people for long. Life found its direction by being among the people. The people were the voice by which a person navigated through each day. Leave your people, and you would have to find another voice.

Leave your *father's household*. Usually, a person would be considered insane to do this. The *father's household* was life's safety net. The family did business together, cared for one another in sickness and old age, picked marriage partners, and guaranteed one another's security. Leave your father's household, and you have violated a key tradition: You do not defy your father's authority.

All these implications sit behind this simple sentence: "The LORD has said to Abram, 'Leave.'" Not a simple decision, is it?

Several centuries ago John Bunyan authored *Pilgrim's Progress*. At the beginning he pictured a tormented man, Pilgrim, who in his dark-forest moment knew that he had lost the straight path.

> I saw a man dressed in clothes which looked like rags. He stood in front of his home, a book in his hand, and he appeared to have a

heavy weight on his back. As I watched him, I saw him open the book and begin to read. But as he read, he wept and shook visibly. Then, suddenly when he could control his emotions no longer, he shouted out, "What shall I do?"

"They [family]," Bunyan wrote, "thought he had suffered something of an emotional breakdown. And since it was evening, they decided that the best thing for their husband and father was a good night's sleep. So, as quickly as possible, they got him to bed."

But it was clear the following morning that Pilgrim needed something more than a night's sleep to calm his spirit.

The family attempted various responses: ridicule, confrontation and argument, and finally, benign neglect. And in the face of such treatment, he increasingly withdrew to his room where he would pray and ponder compassionately on their resistance to this message. Sometimes desperate for personal consolation, he would walk alone in the fields reading and praying. This went on for days.

"Occasionally," Bunyan went on, "he would burst out, 'What must I do to be saved?'" Had he known the answer to his own question, he would have enthusiastically done whatever was necessary.

Watch Pilgrim struggle with leaving on his own journey.

One day Pilgrim was accosted by a stranger named Evangelist. Their conversation initiated his mid-course correction.

"What is it that makes you shout so loudly?" the stranger asked.

"Sir, I have concluded from my reading in this book that I am condemned to die, and after that to come to judgment before God."

"Do you see that narrow gate over there?" Evangelist asked.

"No" was Pilgrim's answer.

"Then do you see the shining light?"

"Yes, I think I do."

"Keep your eyes on that light and head in that direction, and you'll come to a gate. When you get there, knock, and you'll be told what to do."

Bunyan wrote,

> I saw the man begin to run. But he'd not run very far when his wife and children realized what was happening and began to call to him to come back. But the man literally put his fingers in his ears and kept running, shouting at the same time, "Life! Life! Eternal Life!"

Bunyan's description of Pilgrim's *leaving* and breaking the pull of familiar voices around him gets its inspiration from Abram's exit from Ur.

These stories (the biblical Abram and Bunyan's fictional Pilgrim) point to the fact that the first step in any kind of massive life-change is renunciation, *leaving*. But leaving is never easy. A deep, powerful hold, like the law of gravity, must be broken, and it must be broken cleanly.

Here is the first thing that must be examined when a mid-course correction does not last. Did the person in question really ever leave? Often, the answer is no. There is no coincidence, I believe, that the first description of a biblically defined marriage includes the phrase, "a man will *leave* his father and mother" (Gen. 2:24, emphasis mine). We have all learned that a marriage cannot work if the former bonds have not been modified.

Abram's leaving in itself was a process. It is apparent that while he left Ur, he did not leave the influence of Sumer right away. There was a temporary settling in Haran, perhaps the northernmost City of the Mesopotamian confederacy. He'd left, but not *left*.

If I were to hazard a guess why, I'd take a look at Abram's father, Terah. In the last verses of Genesis 11, the text seems to indicate that Terah was out in front, symbolically anyway, of this unique family migration, but this may be the result of political correctness in ancient writings. The elder was always seen to be in charge, whether he was in truth.

Nevertheless, until Terah dies, Abram does not jump off into strange territory as the Voice has called him to do. Then again, the Voice may not have revealed the full extent and scope of the *leaving* God intended for Abram until his father died. We will never be quite sure whether Abram was slow on the pedal to leave or whether he felt obliged to wait until his father was gone. (It is hard not to match him in this part of his story against the disciple who *wanted* to follow Jesus but could not until he buried his father.)

Biblical people who believe strongly in the notion that there is an awakening of faith, a jump-starting, if you please, of the soul, do not adequately appreciate that this concept, sometimes called regeneration, really begins with Abram and not with the writings of Paul. Clearly, Abram would never have *left* Ur if he had not heard a Voice beyond himself ("the LORD had said to Abram") compelling him to break former ties.

In our world of rationality and prescribed sanity, we tend to make fun of people who say that they have heard Voices. We are wary of this notion because we know of situations where people have done violent things because they thought they heard a Voice. We tend to suspect people who explain their behaviors and their opinions as a response to a Voice ("God told me that you were the right woman for me"; "Because I am called, my opinion is the correct one, and all of you are wrong"; "Isn't this a wonderful yacht the Lord gave us?").

But we will have to make our peace with the fact that the biblical notion of life-change begins with a Voice that spoke into the life of this one who was to become the father of all who believe and said, *"Leave."* This Voice ascends above all other voices in Abram's life. The voice of culture, the voice of self-interest, the voice of tradition, the voice of security. *"Leave it all!"* the Voice above all voices says.

When I think of Abram's attempting to respond to this *"Leave!"*

(which comes out of a Voice that no one had ever heard before), I think of our grandchildren in their days of infancy when you say, "Jump!" as you hold your arms open to them. To jump is to leave reliable ground and anticipate that Papa's arms will keep you from a bad fall. Then I think about Lucy in the universally loved *Peanuts* comic strip who is always talking Charlie Brown into placekicking a football that she promises to hold for him. Her "Kick!" is not unlike my "Jump" or the Voice's "Leave." All demand an initial trust that the speaker will be faithful. In Charlie Brown's case, the voice was *never* faithful. Lucy always found a reason to snatch the ball away at the last second and cause Charlie to fall flat on his rear end. Lucy is like the gods of Abram's birth world. Unreliable, petty, and often vindictive.

Don't be surprised, then, that *leaving* took a little time for Abram. But leave he did. Eventually. Which brings me no end of comfort. I would find it hard to relate to an Abram who left *immediately*. I understand the Abram at this end of the twine who hears, stumbles forward a bit, halts, and then heads out again. The game of Mother-may-I has started, and Abram's progress forward will be, on occasion, rather embarrassing.

The journey's destination was a mystery to Abram. "Go to the land I will show you" is a fairly open-ended plan. And if *leaving* is an act of obedience, the willingness to head for an unidentified destination is an act of trust. From beginning to end, Abram is going to learn that a powerful, faith-driven life demands both: total obedience and trust.

The writer of the New Testament book of Hebrews (chap. 11) highlights this mystery about a destination with these words: "By faith Abraham [Abram], when called to go to a place he would later receive as his inheritance, obeyed and went, even though he did not know where he was going . . . He made his home in the promised land like a stranger in a foreign country; he lived in tents" (vv. 8–9). No small matter if you've left a land where you were a person of means, in control of your destiny, known to your people, secure in your customs and culture.

In the final analysis, *leaving* is a letting go of the familiar and the safe. In initiating the thirty-nine-second "burn" that took the *Apollo 13* from one track to another, the astronauts had to believe that the calculations hurriedly done were correct and would line them up for a safe reentry into the earth's atmosphere. Their mid-course correction was a huge decision.

Any of life's mid-course corrections begin with a similar leaving. And the greatest leaving of them all—responding to the Voice that calls into the human heart for reconciliation and communion—is no exception.

It has come to me during the years of my own journey that there is a Leaving (capital *L*) and there are leavings. The first is a personal declaration that I will loosen myself from what has held me in the past; the second is a daily declaration that I will loosen myself from all the things that claw at the soul and threaten to pull it away from God's purposes.

For Abram, his leaving will be vindicated fully and finally when he reaches the mountain. For a moment he will be tested to the core when the Voice asks for far more than just the leaving of his country, his people, and his father's household. That was the past. On the mountain, the Voice will ask for his future: his only son.

Chapter 7

Into the Haze

The news has just broken that an airplane piloted by John F. Kennedy Jr. has gone down in the Long Island Sound. With him in the plane are his wife and his sister-in-law. A famous family once again is beginning to grieve the sudden loss of members of its young generation.

Experts in flying are telling us that one of a pilot's greatest challenges is to fly into an evening haze over water. In a matter of seconds, they say, a flier can become disoriented. He has no idea whether he is in level flight, ascending or descending, banking to the right or left. Only the instruments can indicate the truth, and inexperienced pilots sometimes ignore or distrust them.

This is apparently, according to the experts, what happened to John F. Kennedy Jr. In the haze over Martha's Vineyard, he lost his way.

And this is why the ancients in Abram's day would fear a journey such as the one he has begun. He is traveling into haze. Humanly speaking, he will have only the descriptions of travelers he meets along the way by which to navigate. Who knows how trustworthy a stranger might be? Who knows what dangers he will face? And who knows what resources are necessary to survive?

But a Voice has called him into motion, and it will have to be the

Voice who will lead the way. This is a journey designed to teach faith and bring mid-course correction. When it is complete, Abram will have been given the credentials to be called "the father of all who believe."

ALTAR-BUILDING:
TAKE ONE STEP FORWARD

> Abram traveled through the land . . . The LORD appeared to Abram and said, "To your offspring I will give this land." So he built an altar there to the LORD, who had appeared to him. (Gen. 12:6–7)

From the outset, Abram set a pattern of establishing places where he might be refreshed by the Voice that had called him from his ancestral home. Several times we have references to his building of altars. On other occasions there were visions and appearances in which further information was disclosed to him about his journey on the trail of the twine. Almost always these moments came when Abram had managed to exhaust himself or manipulate himself into near disaster.

An altar was a tiny sanctuary, a piece of consecrated ground in a world of virulent evil, where Abram could worship and receive a refreshing word of promise. Building it was a statement: I set this place apart from all other places as a holy place where God can speak.

And speak God did. At each altar, Abram would learn more of God's purposes for him. The truth was progressively unfolded to him. I have the sense that God could tell Abram only so much at a time. His ability to trust and to handle information was, at first, strictly limited. The fullness of God's plan in its detailed form would have to wait until he was ready.

The hidden purposes of God can be progressively exposed at altars. Some are disclosed quickly; others over a longer period of time. But I want to emphasize that God has purposes for history and for His people that will *never* be revealed this side of heaven.

What Abram needed to know was most often decoded for him at altars. His experience prompts me to take a form of altar-building in my own journey far more seriously.

As I have mused upon the great awakening of Abram, I think I've identified five difficult tests that this man faced. Together they constitute a picture of the first significant life-change all people must contemplate: *a revitalization of spirit* that goes to the core of our being. When it is complete, heaven will say, "Now I know that you fear God."

TEST ONE: SELF-PRESERVATION

Now there was a famine in the land, and Abram went down to Egypt to live there for a while because the famine was severe . . . And when Pharaoh's officials saw her [Sarai], they praised her to Pharaoh, and she was taken into his palace. He treated Abram well for her sake, and Abram acquired sheep and cattle, male and female donkeys, menservants and maidservants, and camels. (Gen. 12:10, 15–16)

If Abram was to be father of all who believe, he would have to deal first with his natural instinct toward self-preservation. On the trail of the twine, Abram reaches Canaan, the promised land, only to face the crisis of a famine. Ignoring the Voice that has called him to this place, he heads southward to Egypt. The Bible will record a number of people who went south to Egypt when times were tough in the promised land. And always they get into trouble.

Abram is a case in point. Arriving in Egypt, he is suddenly sensitive to the issue of his wife's beauty and the fact that Sarai will be attractive to the Egyptians. "They will kill me but will let you live," he tells Sarai. "Say you are my sister, so that I will be treated well for your sake and my life will be spared because of you" (Gen. 12:12–13).

We have words for a man who acts like this. This man, whom we might have found easy to like in the beginning, is revealed as something of a moral coward—at least by our standards. But Abram's world is a tough world, and apparently, men of his time often connived and manipulated their way through life in these ways. Do you want a man like this as the father of your faith? A man whose instinct is first to save himself the minute things become threatening? I think not. "Abram: take two steps backward."

This all goes to suggest that we're watching a man who is a work-in-progress. Perhaps over there on the heavenly side, Abram is already claimed as God's beloved, but on the earthly side, at times, he seems to be a rat. When we read that Sarai is "taken into the palace" while Abram spends his time acquiring "sheep and cattle, male and female donkeys, menservants and maidservants, and camels," we're raising our eyebrows and wondering about this scoundrel.

The truth is that Abram should never have gone to Egypt in the first place. A notable symbol that his life had been fully transformed would have been for him to trust God for day-to-day survival as later generations of Hebrews have to do in the desert.

Of course, in the larger biblical perspective, we wish Abram hadn't lied about Sarai, even though on the basis of a technicality (she is the daughter of his father but not of his mother), he was telling the truth—part of it anyway.

Why is this story here? Perhaps because in the scheme of scriptural revelation, we are supposed to realize that life-change is mostly progressive and often egged on more through defeat and error rather than through the passage of information. The Abram we see in this story is not yet ready for prime time when it comes to being the father of all who believe. He is merely on the way. His awakening is only partial. He trusted enough to *leave* his home base but not enough to put his survival in the midst of famine or a strange country in the hands of God. Don't expect Abram to be consistent in all that he does. He is as jagged as the rest of us. He may have left Sumer, but Sumer has not altogether left him. The man is afraid.

TEST TWO:
BUSINESS DECISIONS

> The land could not support them [Abram and Lot] while they
> stayed together, for their possessions were so great that they were
> not able to stay together. And quarreling arose . . . So Abram said to
> Lot, "Let's not have any quarreling between you and me . . . Is not
> the whole land before you? Let's part company." (Gen. 13:6–9)

The second test of Abram's life-change comes with his relationship to Lot. As I look into the story, it seems almost as if the test is
passed before we even learn of what's to happen.

In Egypt both Abram and Lot, his nephew (or whatever), had gotten obscenely rich. And Pharaoh let him take the loot from the country (a hidden blessing?). But wealth has its traps, and one of them is
the inevitable conflict that seems to arise among the wealthy. Before
long Abram and Lot are having business problems.

We are left to our imaginations here, but I choose to think that
there is no coincidence that Abram is fresh from building an altar and
calling upon the name of the Lord just before this story emerges. The
suggestion appears to be that Abram, starved for a fresh word from
the Voice, has heard, and in the hearing he has gotten his priorities
straightened out.

Neither business nor Lot is to get in the way of the purposes for
which Abram has been called to the promised land. Lot should never
have come along on this journey in the first place (he is clearly a drag
to Abram's spirit). And God never called Abram to the promised land
for the purpose of amassing wealth. At this point, both are therefore a
distraction and must be brought under management.

The answer: a division of the assets and of the organization of the
businesses. "Let's part company," Abram says. "If you go to the left, I'll
go to the right. If you go to the right, I'll go to the left."

I am constrained to suggest that two things are going on here. First, Abram has begun to lean more into the fellowship of God rather than the fellowship of kin (whom he was to leave behind in the first place). Second, Abram is making a decision that is blessedly unbusinesslike. In other words, looking after the business and assuring its prosperity are no longer as important as following the direction in which the Voice is leading him. As the elder, the leader, the one with more power, Abram had the right of choice in this moment. A businesslike decision would have been to take advantage of the right of first choice and to have headed in the direction of the well-watered plain of the Jordan. *Any Middle Easterner can tell you that the choice of the watered plain for your business in contrast to the hill country (dry as can be) is a no-brainer.* That's if you're making your decisions primarily on a business basis. But Abram wasn't! His awakening faith had grown a notch. "Abram: take one step forward."

Lot chose as anyone might have predicted. His was a business decision, and he went for the gold as any young person might who isn't hearing the Voice.

Lot went for profit, and God immediately disclosed to Abram (in Lot's absence, note) that his "profit" would be in offspring "like the dust of the earth" (Gen. 13:16). Go and walk through the land, Abram, the Voice explains. If I were writing the story, I would be tempted, looking toward the moment on the mountaintop, to write, "And Abram feared God just a little bit more."

From that time forth, it seems that Lot is always in trouble but that Abram becomes stronger.

TEST THREE: GENEROSITY AND SECURITY

Then Abram gave him [Melchizedek] a tenth of everything. The king of Sodom said to Abram, "Give me the people and keep the goods for yourself." But Abram said, . . . "I have raised my hand to the LORD, God Most High, Creator of heaven and earth, and have taken an oath that I will accept nothing belonging to you . . . so that you will never be able to say, 'I made Abram rich.'" (Gen. 14:20–23)

In a third incident, we see Abram on the developing edge in his awakening faith once more. Lot and his family, now living in Sodom, are kidnapped by marauding armies, and it appears as if life for them may be over. But Abram, getting word of the demise of Sodom and its king, masses a household of soldiers and engineers a pursuit and rescue of Lot, his possessions, and the booty stolen from the entire city of Sodom.

Naturally, Abram is a hero. As he returns from his expedition with both people and goods, he is met by two "friendly" kings: Melchizedek and, later, the king of Sodom. What he does here is interesting.

To Melchizedek, a strange and mysterious *Older* Testament figure, he offers a tithe of all he has. For reasons that neither the Genesis writer nor other biblical writers who speak of Melchizedek explain, he is seen as God's representative, an extraordinary priestlike figure who receives acknowledgment on behalf of God. The storyteller is content to say, "He was priest of God Most High" (Gen. 14:18), and he was capable of providing Abram with a sense of genuine blessing. The words are significant:

> Blessed be Abram by God Most High,
>> Creator of heaven and earth.
> And blessed be God Most High,
>> who delivered your enemies into your hand. (Gen. 14:19–20)

The Voice has spoken through a person. God is here, and we have a vague sense that Abram is experiencing a moment like the one that Saul of Tarsus will experience when Christ appears to him in the sky.

At this point in Abram's life-change he is perceptive enough to realize that he should give a gift in response. An excellent and significant exchange in a Middle Eastern cultural context. The gift of 10 percent of all Abram has is one of the earliest biblical acknowledgments that God has a claim on all we own and that a tithe is an expression of our understanding that we are merely *stewards* or *managers* of what we have, not owners. Not a particularly American thought.

The incident has not offered all of its lessons, however, until Abram meets the king of Sodom. This man has the greatest reason to be grateful (excepting perhaps Lot and his family, who are strangely absent and silent in this story) to Abram. Abram has saved his city-state; Abram has, in fact, saved his neck.

And Sodom's king is not remiss in offering thankfulness: "Give me the people and keep the goods for yourself."

Go slow here! To Melchizedek, Abram gives. From the king of Sodom, Abram refuses to receive, saying:

> I have raised my hand to the LORD, God Most High, Creator of heaven and earth, and have taken an oath that I will accept nothing belonging to you, not even a thread or the thong of a sandal, so that you will never be able to say, "I made Abram rich." I will accept nothing but what my men have eaten and the share that belongs to the men who went with me . . . Let them have their share. (Gen. 14:22–24)

Bottom line: Abram will take nothing more than expenses. Something has been learned here. Something is different from Abram's experience in Egypt. There he took all he could get. Here he takes nothing. Why?

The message seems to be that Abram has raised the bar of his awakening another notch. He is learning that his life is to be found in alignment with the God behind the Voice. His sojourn in the promised land will no longer be held hostage to the whims or hostilities of people in the land. God alone will sustain him. "Abram: take another two steps forward."

My thoughts go back to a powerful small plane flown by a reasonably competent pilot that goes down in haze. How close Abram came to having a similar experience. But he didn't because those altars make a big difference.

Chapter 8

Learning to Trust

There are few days more memorable in my life than those in which our son and our daughter were born. And close behind those, the days when each of our five grandchildren was placed in my arms to receive Papa's blessing.

But I can't begin to think I am close to the sense of ecstasy that Abram must have felt the day his son Isaac was born. You could say that he'd waited more than ninety years for this moment. Waited in a world where a man's sons were the most important of all treasures.

"Now Sarai was barren; she had no children" (Gen. 11:30). Back at the very beginning of the story, where the trail of the twine began, the Abram and Sarai marriage is marked by infertility. The very fact that it is mentioned gives us a hint that the writer sees this issue as the hinge point of the entire story. In one sense, everything else is a prelude to this one situation that sits at the core of their marriage. It is a near obsession with Abram, an intolerable problem. There must be a solution.

Genesis 15 unpacks an intimate conversation between Abram and the Voice out of heaven that he is beginning to trust. Abram is increasingly free from the gravitational pull of Sumer. He is beginning to think and act like a new man. This Abram would now be virtually unrecognizable to his hometown friends. He is no longer captured by their fate-driven, wheel-like view of history where nothing changes.

This Abram is learning about hope, about trust, about possibilities in the future that his old way of life would have forbidden imagining. He can dare to think that there is a God whose purposes are everlasting and beneficial. This is an Abram learning to think in new ways. His life is changing at the deepest levels.

As Abram enters the gravitational pull of God Most High (the name behind the Voice), there is a conversation between the two. The Bible dates this conversation as "after this," meaning that there is a significant attachment between Abram's conversation with the two kings and what is about to happen in his life on the trail of the twine.

> Do not be afraid, Abram.
> I am your shield [Lot had none],
> your very great reward [others are playing business games].
> (Gen. 15:1)

These words stand alone and would leave us confused if we did not have Abram's response, a sense of what he heard God saying. God speaking of a future: tomorrow resplendent with sons galore, a nation of children comparable to the sands at the shore and the stars of the sky, which is a lot of children!

If Abram had been tested by staying in Canaan (which he originally failed), tested by trusting his life to the protection of God instead of conniving with Sarai on the sister-thing (which he handled poorly), tested by giving to Melchizedek, and not taking money from Sodom's king, here he was being tested by something bigger than all of those combined.

TEST FOUR: SEEKING A SON

The man had no heir. Perhaps this will seem as nothing to a modern generation that feels every liberty in the world to choose not to have children, to even suggest that children are a bother, an encroachment on one's personal freedom, or too much responsibility in a career-driven age.

But to this ancient man, it meant far more than we could ever imagine. From his vantage point, an heir was not only someone who would inherit the family wealth but, far more important, this one would become *the custodian of the family's spirit.* In the son's future life, a father saw his continuing life. And Abram probably thought that way (you could say the concept was in his genes).

Almost all ancients thought this way. It is fair to say that the intimacy a father felt for his son was easily equal to, if not greater than, the intimacy between a husband and a wife. Listen to Jesus say, "I and the Father are one," "He who has seen Me has seen the Father," and "I go about my Father's business." These are not statements unique to Jesus. They are the expressions of father-son intimacy down through the ages. What got Jesus into trouble was not that He said them, but that all people knew which *Father* He was talking about. Had He said it about Joseph, the people would have shrugged their shoulders and asked what the big deal was.

But Abram had no son to be "one" with, no one with whom to share a common male identity, no one to participate with in the family business. He must have felt rather foolish listening to a Voice that promised him a nation of countless heirs when he and Sarai could not produce even one child.

For a time Abram took this matter of an heir into his own hands. He liked what the Voice was saying (your offspring shall be as the number of the stars), but he lacked confidence that the God of the Voice could make it happen. His ancestral gods had been rather undependable, and although this God had a good track record so far, why should he push his luck?

Abram decided to help God out. In this instance he is a very modern man. He lied in Egypt, and now he manipulates the circumstances. "Abram: three steps backward."

Abram, now the "helper" of God, has followed old cultural habits and appointed Eliezer, apparently a slave (perhaps a very, very nice slave), to be his official heir. In the traditions of the time, that was not an unheard-of gesture. It's just not worthy of one who will, one day, be designated as the father of all who believe. What does this version of the man have to say to us about the actual depth of Abram's midcourse correction?

The Voice: "This man will not be your heir, but a son coming from your own body will be your heir" (Gen. 15:4). To an old man who, with his wife, has waited a lifetime with agony through virtually every female cycle to see if there was a pregnancy, to a man who knows (at least in an ancient sense) that his own sperm count is zero (Paul: "he faced the fact that his body was as good as dead" [Rom. 4:19]), to a man who knows that he hasn't many more years left, this is an incredible statement.

"O Sovereign LORD, how can I know that I will gain possession of it?" (Gen. 15:8).

It's a reasonable and predictable question. The question of a man whose awakening to life-change is being tested to the breaking point and beyond. He really is saying, "No way!" One thinks of similar questions from other biblical people whose faith was also being tested. Mary to the angel: "How shall these things happen since I've never slept with a man?" A woman whom Jesus meets at Jacob's well in Samaria: "How can you give me water since you have nothing to draw water with?" The disciples of our Lord: "We have only five loaves of bread and two fish. How can we feed these people unless we go and buy food for them?" All good people, but their faith for greater possibilities is in the tadpole stage. Abram fits this description perfectly. The Voice has said that a son will come the most natural way. Abram really doesn't believe.

There follows an ancient ritual, one that Abram would understand even if we might not. A heifer, a goat, a ram, a dove, and a pigeon are collected for a special covenantal ceremony. In such a setting the Voice will affirm the promise in a visual way that might conceivably break down the doubts, fears, and uncertainties of this man who is awakening to a life of faith. The larger animals are cut in two, halved. During the ritualistic placement of the sacrificial event, birds try to eat away at the carcasses, and Abram (the Bible describes this) frantically runs about shooing them off. Nothing will destroy this covenantal ceremony if Abram has anything to do with it. He will go to any extent, to any length, to assure that the promise will be affirmed and kept.

"As the sun was setting, Abram fell into a deep sleep, and a thick and dreadful darkness came over him" (Gen. 15:12). The Voice was once again very present. The promise is reiterated: There will be descendants, many in number, enslaved for a time in Egypt. But they will come out. In other words, they will have their leaving too: "You, however, will go to your fathers in peace and be buried at a good old age" (Gen. 15:15). These were wonderful words of life to an old traveler like Abram. He'd left Sumer in hope of hearing this.

There was the further promise of a homeland for Abram's descendants, and then the Voice was silent. "One step forward, Abram."

Unfortunately, the story is not finished. From this experience of incredible power and force, Abram would once again take a step backward on the trail of the twine. Almost instantly (although time must have passed), we are told that Abram listens to another "voice," that of his wife, Sarai, who suggests that an heir might be produced through the surrogate mother process. And here we move on to the story of Hagar, Sarai's maidservant.

Now Sarai, Abram's wife, had borne him no children. But she had an Egyptian maidservant named Hagar; so she said to Abram, "The LORD has kept me from having children. Go, sleep with my maidservant; perhaps I can build a family through her." (Gen. 16:1–2)

If going to Egypt had gotten Abram into trouble, that was nothing compared to this. Hagar conceived, and there was a short period of delight until the consequences set in.

Everyone is a loser in this story. The mother-to-be begins to treat Sarai with disdain. One can imagine the naïve Abram saying to his wife, "What's the big deal? If she insists on acting like a jerk, ignore her. Don't make waves! After all she's carrying our baby."

Advice like this does not help Sarai. Soon there is big trouble in the household. Sarai blames Abram (the reverse of Adam's blaming of Eve) for what is happening. Abram shirks off any responsibility for the deed and permits Sarai to do as she wishes, which is not a helpful solution. A shot of wisdom would have helped.

Hagar, now at the mercy of Sarai, is abused to the extent that she runs away, only to return by the encouragement of an angel. But the damage has been done. And some say that the enmity between the sons of Ishmael (the Arabs) and the sons of the future Isaac (the Jews), so vitriolic until this day, began at that point. I do not find that hard to believe. There are awesome consequences whenever we make stupid attempts to help God out in the fulfilling of His promises. Abram was eighty-six years old at the time of this fiasco.

"Abram: take two more steps backward."

How does such an ancient episode, one whose details seem unthinkable in a modern world such as ours, speak into our time? Does it seem possible that we, too, may have similar obsessions and preoccupations that blind us to God's purposes? I am left a bit uncomfortable as I think back across the years when my trust in God's ways was far too small to wait upon Him for deliverance or for guidance. I have not been a lot different from this frantic older couple who, when the pressure was on, drew upon every thing they ever knew back in the days of Sumer to hurry up the ultimate dream of their lives to have a son.

FROM ABRAM TO ABRAHAM

Thirteen years later, it was apparently decided in heaven that Abram had been stretched long enough in his progressive awakening to faith and trust in God Most High: "When Abram was ninety-nine years old, the LORD appeared to him and said, 'I am God Almighty; walk before me and be blameless. I will confirm my covenant between me and you and will greatly increase your numbers'"(Gen. 17:1–2).

"Abram fell facedown," the writer reported. A gesture of complete submission. This is the posture of a man who has learned the hard way to fear God. It has taken more than thirty years perhaps for this moment to come. The sovereign God has looked into Abram's heart and seen life-change of such significance and authenticity that he is prepared to anoint him as (Paul's words) the father of all who believe.

A name change occurs. In ancient culture, such a change of names signifies a change of relationship, a sense of change of the quality of the person, an extending of great honor. Abram's name (esteemed father) is now to be Abraham (the father of countless people).

God said, "I will bless her [Sarah—her name is also changed] and will surely give you a son by her. I will bless her so that she will be the mother of nations; kings of peoples will come from her" (Gen. 17:16). Does Abraham get it? "Abraham fell facedown; he laughed and said to himself, 'Will a son be born to a man a hundred years old? Will Sarah bear a child at the age of ninety?' And Abraham said to God, 'If only Ishmael might live under your blessing!'" (Gen. 17:17–18).

Can you see yourself saying these things to God? What Abraham says, we often think. How gracious of the biblical writers to offer us such insights into great men who were dragged kicking and screaming along their trail of twine. How revealing that even after these many years, an admired man still doubts and actually laughs, that he still thinks he knows better than God almighty. And how kind of God not to lose His patience with such a disrespectful Abraham.

As I said, the story has its jagged edges. The laughing, doubting, know-it-all Abram of yesterday is, a day later, circumcising his entire family—a physical ritual that makes one thing clear: Abraham (including his family) is now God's man. There's no turning back. The break with the Sumerian past is complete; *the awakening has had its full effect.* Abraham knows in whom he trusts. He will live in God's way. The man has truly *left!*

This is the person who has begun to acquire a vital optimism, a hope in the hidden promises of God. "Abraham, take a giant step forward."

TWO TRAILS

Before the final test of Abraham's awakening, the reader of his story is jolted back to the world of Lot. The tale of Lot is instructive because it gives us a vivid picture of two men: one who had an awakening to faith and another who, for all purposes, did not. For sure, we have a mysterious allusion to "righteous Lot" in the New Testament (2 Peter 2:7), but if we stick to the Genesis story, the man just doesn't look good. Unlike Abraham, he had not bothered to discern the Voice. When he'd been in Abraham's world, he'd apparently acknowledged Abraham's God. But left alone, he played the chameleon and pursued whatever it took to acquire wealth and the good life. That's about the best we can say. His personal trail of twine goes downhill and ends, as far as we can see, in general disgrace and total loss of everything.

The story of Lot's exit from Sodom is well known. Heavenly visitors had reached his home to warn him to flee before the city faced its final judgment. Lot, smart enough to know a genuine warning when he heard one, had rushed to his sons-in-law to convince them to leave with him: "So Lot went out and spoke to his sons-in-law, who were pledged to marry his daughters. He said, 'Hurry and get out of this place, because the LORD is about to destroy the city!' But his sons-in-law thought he was joking" (Gen. 19:14).

It occurs to me that the sons-in-law might have profited from hearing Abraham's story of what it means to leave a familiar place. Unlike him, *they weren't leaving*. Like residents living on an East Coast beach who are told to evacuate in the face of an oncoming hurricane but will not, they don't believe him. Which is to suggest that Lot's testimony of faith in the Voice that had moved Abraham so powerfully must be totally unreliable.

Even Lot is not so sure that the messengers of the Voice are to be trusted. Watch him waver:

> With the coming of dawn, the angels urged Lot, saying, "Hurry! Take [your family] . . . or you will be swept away when the city is punished." When he hesitated, the men grasped his hand and the hands of his wife and of his two daughters and led them safely out of the city, for the LORD was merciful to them. (Gen. 19:15–16)

Lot's wife, whose name is never mentioned, is too wedded to Sodom. *Leaving* is not in her blood either. When the city falls under the judgment of God's anger, "Lot's wife looked back, and she became a pillar of salt" (Gen. 19:26).

Lot and his two daughters ended up in a cave in the mountains. Other than a brief reference to him in the New Testament, we never hear of Lot again. As he disappears off the scene we are told of evenings of debauchery in which his daughters seduce him and become pregnant.

Why has the Genesis writer told us about these things? This is my guess: The writer wants us to see two trails of twine, neither a particularly pretty sight. Nevertheless, one trail of twine leads forward under the guidance of the God of hidden purposes. Of course, there are humiliating detours where the traveler has chosen alternative paths. But this man, Abraham, is getting where God has called him to go.

The other trail leads toward oblivion. It is the track of a man who may have left the geographical Sumer but never left the spiritual one. At every turn in the trail he has resorted to the ways and means of the culture of his birth. And now he has inherited the consequences of a bundle of bad choices.

Abraham is not far from his day on the mountain when we shall see him in the glory of his mid-course correction. But Lot has hit bottom. And we never learn another thing about what happened to him.

TEST FIVE: FAILURE

There is one more hiccup in the trail of the twine of Abraham's life. And to be honest, I would find it easy to join with the biblical critics who find this story too similar to the Sarai-in-Egypt story and suggest that it doesn't belong here. But what if it does?

Believe it or not, Abraham tries to pull off the Sarah-is-my-sister story once again. In a strange part of the promised land, he runs into Abimelech, a local king who is apparently a bit fearsome (but certainly not to be compared to the Pharaoh in Egypt).

"I said to myself, 'There is surely no fear of God in this place, and they will kill me because of my wife.' Besides, she really is my sister" (Gen. 20:11–12). This will be Abraham's explanation to Abimelech about why he tried to pass off his ninety-something-year-old wife as his sister. Stretches my credulity.

What's the message here? Let me suggest one. No matter how far, how deep, how high a man has gone in the awakening journey of faith, he is never far from a fall off the edge. In truth, Abraham is a fearful man. And we must not let his impressive journey through the land of Canaan make us forget that down deep at soul-level there remains a man who can stoop pretty low in a fearful moment.

One thinks of other surprise moments in the lives of notable biblical personalities when, at the moment we might have expected their best, they gave their worst. David at the height of his glory tempted toward Bathsheba; Jonah, apparently a powerful prophet, kidding himself into thinking he can escape to Tarshish; Simon Peter promising heroism and sinking into cowardice. In truth, none of us is ever far from a great fall.

"Abraham: take ... Oh, forget it!"

My friend Ben Patterson has told a wonderful story out of his life in the book *Waiting*. He and three good friends had begun a day's climb up Mount Lyell in Yosemite National Park. "Two of us," Patterson writes, "were experienced mountaineers; two of us were not. I was not one of the experienced two ... the climb to the top and back was to take the better part of a day due, in large part, to the difficulty of the glacier one must cross to get to the top."

Soon after the climb began, the two sets of men were separated as the more proficient hikers moved on ahead: "Being competitive by nature, I began to look for shortcuts I might be able to take to beat [the men ahead] to the top. I thought I saw one to the right of an outcropping of rock—so up I went, deaf to the protests of my companion."

The fact that the most experienced climbers had not chosen this way did not occur to Patterson:

It should have, for thirty minutes later, I was trapped in a cul-de-sac of rock atop the Lyell Glacier, looking down several hundred feet of a sheer slope of ice, pitched at a forty-five degree angle. It is one thing to climb up a glacier, and quite another to climb down or traverse it. I was only about ten feet from the safety of a rock, but one little slip and I wouldn't stop sliding until I landed in the valley floor some fifty miles away.

On several occasions we see Abraham and Lot in similar predicaments. Perhaps we can begin to discern that in such moments their emerging faith is powerfully road-tested. In Lot's case, each test ends in failure. Thus, we should not be surprised when his life ends in disintegration and disgrace.

But Abraham's story is different.

Ben Patterson, stranded on the Lyell Glacier, describes how his two friends came to his rescue:

> Standing on the rock I wanted to reach, one of them leaned out and used an ice axe to chip two little footsteps in the glacier. Then he gave me the following instructions: "Ben, you must step out from where you are and put your foot where the first foothold is. When your foot touches it, without a moment's hesitation swing your other foot across and land it on the next step. When you do that, reach out and I will take your hand and pull you to safety."

There was one other instruction: "As you step across, do not lean into the mountain! If anything, lean out a bit. Otherwise, your feet may fly out from under you and you will start sliding down." Patterson goes on to say that this last piece of advice caused him some deep thought:

> When I am on the edge of a cliff, my instincts are to lie down and hug the mountain, to become one with it, not to lean away from it. But that was what my good friend was telling me to do as I stood trembling on that glacier. I looked at him real hard. I searched my memory for anything I might have done to him in the past for him

to harbor any ill will toward me. Was there any reason, any reason at all, that I should not trust him?

This is Abraham on his own glacier. The man is in his nineties. The Voice—the Lord, God Most High, God Almighty—has permitted events on the journey that bring him out on slippery ice. Will he continue to listen, or will he return to his instincts?

Those who ask if the way of life-change will grow easier as time goes by might profit from Abraham's story to date. The answer is no: Life-change does not get easier. It may grow more difficult as the issues and the questions grow greater. In the early years, mid-course corrections involved change of habits, adjustment of a personality, the building of a reputation, the quality of relationships. In later years, the issues along the way will involve facing death or disability, surrendering control, fearing abandonment.

So, does life-change get easier, Abraham? No, he may answer. And then he might add, But the Voice gets louder and easier to trust.

Ben Patterson continues:

So for a moment, based solely on what I believe to be true about the good will and good sense of my friend, I decided to say no to what I felt, to stifle my impulse to cling to the security of the mountain, to lean out, step out, and traverse the ice to safety. It took less than two seconds to find out if my faith was well-founded. It was.

Chapter 9

SCARS ON MY FAITH

In the one-hundredth year of his life, Sarah, through the graciousness of God, made Abraham a father. In the words of the biblical writer, "The LORD did for Sarah what he had promised" (Gen. 21:1).

"God has brought me laughter," Sarah said. "Who would have said to Abraham that Sarah would nurse children? Yet I have borne him a son in his old age" (Gen. 21:6–7).

I feel glad just writing these words.

The loss of vital optimism that had threatened to overcome Abraham in earlier days as he and Sarah moved past the childbearing years is now reversed. These two have what was the most important thing to every ancient family. They have their son. The family line endures.

It would be nice if the story would begin to wind down with a tidy conclusion. You'd like to know that Sarah and Hagar made peace, that Ishmael was welcomed to the larger family with enthusiasm. You'd feel better if Abraham took charge of the situation and brought it to an honorable resolution.

But the story of Hagar and Ishmael ends in (my opinion) a messy fashion. There is a mean-spiritedness in Sarah toward Hagar and her son. And Abraham, with the mysterious permission (hidden purposes?) of God, sends Hagar away from the family.

The good news is that we are told of God's care and affection for Ishmael and his mother.

We like our religious heroes to reach a standard of near perfection. That cannot be said, however, of Abraham. The biblical writer seems bent on giving us a man whose passions, whose faults and flaws, whose doubts and fears, are like ours.

When we elevate people, then and now, into celebrity status, we serve them and ourselves poorly. We forget that we are all born broken, and we remain basically broken all of our days. The best we can hope for is that the journey of awakening faith will see a constant state of life-change happening from day to day, for the God of Abraham is the God of all others who seek to hear His Voice.

We know nothing about Isaac's earliest years in the Abrahamic family. His growth as a boy is left a mystery. Judging from his one brief interchange with his father on the way up the mountain ("Father, where is the lamb?"), he seems a rather compliant child who knows his place and trusts his father's judgment. His life passes by quickly in the Genesis account. We know that at the age of forty, he married Rebekah, clearly a very strong woman. We are informed that they raised two sons, Jacob and Esau, and that Isaac in his old age, now a weak and blind man close to death, blew the traditional blessing of the firstborn son badly and designated Jacob rather than Esau as his primary heir.

And yet all of this, the Bible will teach, comes under the hidden purposes of God.

This brings us back to where we began, on a mountaintop at the end of the trail of twine that began back in Sumer years before. A man has taken his only son, Isaac, his most prized possession, his only hope, to the top of the mountain.

Was there ever a moment during that climb when Abraham was

tempted to defiant thought? Could the words ever have formed in his head, *Well this God has finally shown His true colors. He is no different from all the gods of my ancestors after all. For thirty years He has dangled this marvelous hope before me, permitted me to become attached to my son, and now He wants him back?* If Jesus would say, "Why have you forsaken Me?" would Abraham have been tempted to cry out, "How could You do this to me?"

Perhaps that thought was there. There's no way to know. But we do know several things, and they flow from Abraham's actions. Here is life-change, the result of a great awakening in this man's life.

MID-COURSE CORRECTION: THE EVIDENCE

This man had learned obedience. He'd learned it way back when the Voice had called him to *leave* Sumer. This man had learned trust. That was settled back in the day when he placed his security in the hands of the Voice and permitted Lot to run away with the best parts of the family business. And this man had learned stewardship of all things, perhaps beginning on the day when he gave a tithe to Melchizedek and refused to take booty from the king of Sodom.

This last chapter in Abraham's life began with the comment: "Some time later God tested Abraham" (Gen. 22:1). In a sense testings (the five I've already highlighted) had been going on for years. But this was the test that ascended over and above all others. I have no doubt that it would have been a colossal failure if Abraham had not gone through the previous difficult experiences. All the events we have looked at previously have lined up like dots pointing to the ultimate mountaintop moment in which Abraham was able to give evidence to the faith that he feared God.

As I retrace the twinelike trail of Abraham's journey back from the mountaintop, I find myself breathless at the depth and breadth of the story. This man was a champion. The courage to *leave;* the hard choices that sometimes he made and sometimes did not make; the doubt and the feelings of anxiety; the darkness that must have overcome his soul the night before he ascended the mountain.

But his mid-course correction was real, solid, deep, broad, tested. Life-change had happened.

E. Stanley Jones, writing in his mid-eighties, looks back across the trail of twine that marks his life. "There are scars on my faith," he writes,

> but underneath those scars there are no doubts. He [Christ] has me with the consent of all my being and with the corroboration of all my life. The song I sing is a life song. Not the temporary exuberance of youth that often fades when middle and old age set in with their disillusionment and cynicisms—the days when one says, "I have no pleasure in them." No, I'm eighty-three, and I'm more excited today about being a Christian than I was at eighteen when I put my feet upon the way.

There were scars on Abraham's faith. Scars accumulated in leaving his home, scars gathered in Egypt, scars grown as he attempted to solve his fertility problems in his own way. There were scars gained in his more noble moments—the decision to part ways with Lot, to refuse ample rewards from the king of Sodom—and scars that mounted up on his way to the ultimate place of sacrifice. Scars but, finally, no doubts.

In another place I have written of a morning spent with a young South African man who had spent five years in prison as a political prisoner in the old apartheid government. I wrote about how much I had come to admire his character and nobility of spirit. I was so impressed that I found myself thinking after I'd left him, *If I could be like that at the price of five years in prison, I'd seriously consider it.*

Now I find myself saying something similar in light of Abraham's story. If I could experience life-change to the extent that he did and become the father of those who believe, I would gladly travel his trail of twine. Or would I?

Chapter 10

CONVERSATION WITH A CHAMPION

A journal entry of mine from two years ago reads:

> Your conversion is not deep enough; it must descend to the depths of your soul where it can reach the embedded powers of evil.

> Your conversion is not long enough; it must be in continuous motion all the days of your life.

> Your conversion is not social enough; it must connect you with the community of converted people who have much to teach you.

> Your conversion is not rugged enough; it must demonstrate its capacity to make a difference in the larger world.

> Your conversion is not high enough; it must be filled with aspiration to commune with the living God.

> Your conversion is not futuristic enough; it must be bathed in the expectation of seeing the Christ who shall come in glory.

A student of theology will want to remind me that *conversion* is, first, a word that describes the adoption of a person, by grace, into the family of God. From this perspective one is completely converted from being a child of the world to a child of heaven. This is conversion as it is celebrated in the timeless expanse of heaven. It is the great mid-course correction.

But *conversion* must be appreciated from another, time-space–oriented perspective. For conversion also identifies the experience of daily life-change under the influence of Christ's power. "We . . . are being transformed," Paul wrote, "into his likeness with ever-increasing glory" (2 Cor. 3:18), which takes place in the days, weeks, and months of living.

In this second sense one can understand why E. Stanley Jones would call himself "a Christian-in-the-making." Being converted, transformed, every day. There is humility in his phrase that many biblical people ought to contemplate. A holy man took the thought a step further when asked if he was a follower of Christ. "I am not the one to answer that question," he said, "but I have seen a few who are."

Both conversions—the first instant and complete, and the second processive (from the word *process*) and, frankly, quite ragged—are initiated by the combustion of God's grace and our faith. In grace God acts; in faith we respond. This is Abraham's story, and it is mine.

Don Snyder is author of a fascinating book called *Cliff Walk*, published in the late 1990s. Snyder, a young family man, had been a soon-to-be-tenured literature professor at Colgate University but awakened one day to the announcement that he was being terminated because of economic downsizing. His teaching days at Colgate, he was informed, would be finished with the school year.

Like most fired professionals, Snyder was incredulous. He had been named teacher of the year by the students. How could he be let go? Surely, he assumed, the termination notice was a bureaucratic mistake and would soon be rectified. But it wasn't. It had never occurred to Snyder that his career wouldn't go anywhere but upward from Colgate to other schools of even greater esteem.

Snyder's book is about *leaving*. Leaving not only a university, but also a profession and a way of life. In leaving, Snyder discovered far more about himself than if he had stayed. *Cliff Walk* describes the transformation of a man's life from professor to hourly construction worker and painter. Like the Mother-may-I life of Abraham, Snyder also knew the forward and then backward steps of a major life-change. His book describes the journey.

There is a passage in *Cliff Walk* where Snyder recounts his decision to discard his working library, which he had used as a professor. In a sense it was the moment when he actually broke with the old way and accepted the reality of the new. A portrait of *conversion* is being painted here:

> I got some trash bags from the kitchen and began going through all my books, separating the ones that I'd written in. But soon I decided to put them all in trash bags, along with more than a dozen spiral notebooks that contained the notes for my lectures.
>
> Then to the town dump, the trunk of his car full of books.
>
> I was the first car there, waiting outside the gates when they opened. "Whatcha got there?" the toothless man in charge of the landfill asked.
>
> "An old life," I said.

Directed to an open fire, Snyder began to throw his books on the flames. One by one the books fed the flames: Emily Dickinson, Herman Melville, Arthur Miller, and a mass of others. Snyder had indeed *left* an old way of life. (I just wish I could have been there to rescue the books from the fire.)

And that was exactly what Abraham faced as he headed north and west from Haran, the last major city of the Sumerian culture. Everything that had defined his way of life—language, customs, status, connection—left behind. *Leave* in this case is a word of great finality.

There is something very special about sitting with an older man or woman who has aged with grace and has much wisdom to impart to a younger generation. Since such people seem few and far between, we long to hear them tell their stories so that we can draw operating principles of life for the present. He is a fool who does not take advantage of such opportunities.

One's imagination runs wild at the thought of sitting at a table with Abraham and Sarah in their last years. Coffee has been served, and talk veers toward the nostalgic. The great leaving from Ur is now years and years in the past. The altars, the embarrassing interlude in Egypt, the struggles with nephew Lot and the miniwars Abraham had fought are now dim memories. And so is the heart-stopping moment on the mountain in Moriah.

Here are two people whose lives have been transformed to the very core of their being. If the word *conversion* applies to anyone, it applies to them.

In a modern setting, we'd ask Abraham if he had any pictures of those early days. Had he recorded his thoughts in a journal? What did he remember about Sumer? We'd want to know from Sarah how it felt to be wrenched from her home, to be dragged on a journey without knowing where she was going, to be put in the middle between Pharaoh and the finagling Abraham. And we'd be curious about the courage it took to split the family business with Lot and take what seemed to be the lesser share. Along the way, we'd hope that they would tell the story behind the birth of Isaac.

In asking such questions, we would really be asking: *What does a journey of faith look like? What did it take for the two of you to be so thoroughly and completely transformed?*

If Abraham were to answer, I think he'd start with the Voice that went to his heart and thrived there. A Voice—that's what it was. He had nothing else to go on except the Voice.

Well, did it come to him, we might ask, like the sound that came

102

to Charlton Heston's Moses in *The Ten Commandments*? Loud, intrusive, reverberating as if in an echo chamber? Or was it a quiet voice, lodged deep, deep in the recesses of an inner part of Abraham that he had not known existed? We do not know and wish we did.

We know that a Voice spoke to Noah. But that's all. We know a Voice spoke to Moses out of a burning bush. A Voice reassured his successor, Joshua. There was a Voice in Samuel's time, in Isaiah's, in Jeremiah's, in Paul's. And we know of a Voice that spoke to Jesus, saying some of the most tender words ever heard: "You are my Son, whom I love" (Mark 1:11).

Abraham nods. He is acquainted with their experiences. "I know that Voice well," he says pensively. But he never does tell us how the Voice spoke into his life. There's simply a certainty that it did and that he heard.

What was there about the Voice that compelled Abraham to pay attention to it? As far as we know, no one else in this period of history but Abraham had heard the Voice. *And what had Abraham done to deserve to hear it?* we ask respectfully. We have no historical data on that, we say.

Abraham shakes his head and smiles. He, too, has wondered many times. He is quite aware, he says, that his life offered nothing that would have made him more deserving than anyone else. That he was chosen is as puzzling to him as all the other purposes in the journey. But he seems comfortable with this.

"You moderns," he says, "are convinced that there is a rational answer to every question. Even those of you who claim that you walk in faith. You just don't know how to accept the mysterious ways of heaven. Let God be God. He has small and large purposes that are often hidden from our eyes. In time, they will be revealed. Today we know a little, not much. Someday we shall know it all. Then I'll be able to answer your question."

It's true. Millennia later, we know much more about that Voice than did Abraham. We know the Voice to be *Logos*, the Word of God, the God above all gods. We know what Abraham progressively learned, that this was the Voice of God Most High, God Almighty. We have come to realize what Abraham would learn in a slow and painful way: something of the character of that Voice. We take some things for granted that Abraham struggled to master all of his life. Namely, that promises spoken out of heaven would be promises kept, that directions given would be reliable, that there was such a thing as a future, and that its possibilities were unlimited.

As Abraham talks on, you realize that there are secrets in this relationship with heaven that he himself cannot explain. He has experienced something glorious, and much of it defies words. As a battle-scarred soldier is reluctant to speak of combat experiences with anyone except those who were there, so Abraham seems reticent to explain everything. It's almost as if he is saying, "You had to have been there."

As the conversation moves forward, I find myself thinking in another part of my head, *Does the Voice that spoke to this man speak to us today?* I answer to myself, *Without a doubt!* God Most High still speaks with an unaltered agenda. The issue is still obedience, still trust, still stewardship.

More than a century ago, John Henry Newman wrote of the Voice,

> He speaks forthrightly in larger and broader ways than Abraham could ever have imagined. He is still here; He still whispers to us, He still makes signs to us. But His voice is too low, and the world's din is too loud, and His signs are so covert, and the world is so restless, that it is difficult to determine when He addresses us, and what He says.

The Voice speaks to us through a grand creation—the heavens and an earth whose systemic life continually boggles the minds of all who study it. Pity those who limit themselves to a mere study of its forms and connections and call this science. For all of its marvelous brilliance, science is merely a starting point in the hearing of God's Voice in creation.

The spiritual masters have, for centuries, told us of the ways in which God speaks in creation. As astronomers search for places in the world where the light and pollution of modern cities will not obscure their view of the heavens, so holy people in each generation have sought quiet places. They have learned that one must regularly step away from the noises and distraction of modernity in order to hear the omnipresent Voice that calls to the soul and prompts an awareness of the majesty and glory of God the Creator.

I am reminded as our visit continues that Abraham never had the chance to hear the even more expansive Voice as it comes to us through Holy Scripture, the record of God's dealings with His people over the centuries. We have heard the thunderous Voice as it rattles our bones through the message of the prophets; he has not. We have been quieted by the soothing, mothering tones of the Voice as it has drawn us to comfort and protection in the Psalms. Abraham isn't acquainted with that. We know the ups and downs of the worshiping generations that came after Abraham; we possess the stories of the great saints. Abraham would like to know these things, but doesn't. And we have the teaching of apostles who have summed up the long record of what heaven has said and revealed to us the difference it can make in our lives. Abraham made that wild journey without the benefit of all we know.

It occurs to me that Abraham most likely could never conceive that the Voice to which he responded would one day become a man like him and like us. And for a time the Voice would live among us as flesh and blood. The Voice, now clothed in the person of One called Jesus, would live the routine life of a laboring person, know what it was to care for His mother, experience the insults and ridicule of those who didn't like Him, face the anger of those who felt uncomfortable or defiant with His insights.

Could Abraham appreciate the story of the Cross, of death and resurrection, of the ascension of Jesus into heaven? Would he begin to make connections between the moment when he was asked to take "your only son, the son whom you love" to the mountain and the Voice whose "beloved Son" was taken to a place called Calvary where a sacrifice of immense cost actually did happen?

Abraham might only guess that the Voice he heard would one day be in all biblical people in the form of the Holy Spirit. And as he had been led throughout a strange land, so his progeny in faith would be led through other promised lands of their own—in the marketplace, in the community, in the home.

Because I am captivated by the subject of mid-course corrections—how the lives of people are transformed—I want to ask Abraham what he thinks of the way the Voice of heaven has reshaped his life, given him a vital optimism his people in the past had never known.

Abraham's new life of faith was built in tough places, he says. Learning and growing never took place on sites set aside for religious purposes. But on roads, in cities, in the desert, in the mountains. His faith, he goes on to say, was forged in the company of tough people who sometimes tried to cheat him and defeat him.

What he learned was not communicated in a special antiseptic vocabulary. He learned in the vocabulary and the thought forms of the day. He admits that he cried a lot, that there were moments when he was paralyzed in doubt and fear. "But the lessons stuck," he says.

I think to myself that his experiences are a precedent for the modern church to consider. We are too often tempted by the seductions of an institutional life that calls its people inside the walls where faith is formed in the context of religious programs and services. When this is what happens, we should not be surprised when people possess a limpid faith hardly capable of usefulness in a larger, real world where places are indeed tough and people even tougher.

Listen to the prayers of the clergy and ask yourself if Abraham would have been comforted by what he might hear had he stopped off at most of our churches along the way.

"Abraham," one of us says, "you've spent the last many years having your life scoured from the inside to the outside. Looking back over these challenging times, how would you like to have been prayed for? I need to know because I'm acquainted with a lot of people facing realities similar to yours."

The aged man thinks for a moment and then forms a response. He would have wished prayers, he says, for wisdom to make gutsy business decisions such as the one he had to make in connection with Lot and his people. He would have loved intercessions for courage as he went out to face hostile warlords and small-town kings. And he would have profited from a plea to God for patience as he waited for a son.

And then he adds: "I would have given anything if someone had interceded for me on the way as I took my son to the mountaintop. No one will ever know how close I was to breaking that day." After a thoughtful pause, he speaks again: "Have you ever asked yourself if there are not people going to similar mountaintops every day to offer up whatever their 'Isaac' is? Because my 'Isaac' could be another person's career, his health, everything he defines as security.

"My dear brother . . ." There is a pause as he leans forward and puts his hand on mine. ". . . every person, including you, will sooner or later be summoned to the mountaintop."

I think of a recent climb to the summit of a high mountain. There at the top was a cairn, a pile of rocks, each of which was placed there by a climber who had been there before me. As I placed my rock with the others, I felt a strange and mystical fellowship with those who had pushed themselves, as I had, to reach the summit.

I am beginning to see Abraham in a new light. And with him, all the others who have gone to the mountaintop where faith has been tested. I am now beginning to understand that I, too, may be called there for similar purposes. I like to think that I would count it a privilege to add my rock to the pile they have already made in testimony to the faithfulness of the One who calls.

We continue to sit at the table listening to Abraham and his good wife, Sarah, reflect on the past. We seize upon every word these experts on the subject of mid-course correction have to offer.

I know I must listen intently because I am fresh from writing in my own journal about how much I wish for my life to experience the enlargement of soul that these two have clearly experienced.

"Just a few more minutes, Abraham? Are you tired, old man? Have you left anything out?"

Abraham raises the issue of obedience. Looking into our world, he reminds me that obedience is a subject in decline. "Your age," he says, "knows relatively little about surrendering to God's purposes. You are confused about authority and submission. The people of your time pride themselves on their defiance; they seem unwilling to bow the knee to anyone. Even God Almighty."

Abraham smiles then and admits that obedience was not his strong suit either. To leave and travel in a direction dictated by a Voice? To seek higher ground when the lower (Lot's ground) would have been more profitable? To wait and wait and wait for a son when there were other means? To . . . offer . . . up . . . a . . . son? No, he says, it was hard. And it must be hard now for you and your people, he acknowledges.

"Nevertheless, ready obedience to the Voice of the Lord when you are called to leave, to grow comfortable with His hidden purposes, is the beginning of true transformation of life." This is Abraham's bottom line.

I must say that I hear Abraham talking about a kind of faith not much in vogue in my time. We love the words of a comforting, soothing God, a God who easily gives in and asks very little. But this is not the God of Abraham. I think the man would have been quite at home with the somewhat violent perspective that the seventeenth-century poet John Donne had,

> Batter my heart, three-personed God, for you
> As yet but knock, breathe, shine, and seek to mend;
> That I may rise, and stand, o'erthrow me, and bend
> Your force to break, blow, burn, and make me new.
> I, like an usurped town, to another due,
> Labour to admit you, but Oh, to no end.
> Reason, your viceroy in me, me should defend,
> But is captived, and proves weak or untrue.
> Yet dearly I love you, and would be loved fain,
> But am betrothed unto your enemy:
> Divorce me, untie or break that knot again,
> Take me to you, imprison me, for I,
> Except you enthrall me, never shall be free,
> Nor ever chaste, except you ravish me.

Batter me? Overthrow me? Break me? Imprison me? Ravish me? Donne and Abraham would understand this sort of language. For the Voice, God Most High, to have truly brought their lives to high transformation, this is what it would have taken.

And then, Abraham says, there is trust that follows on the heels of obedience. He had failed to trust in the Voice at the time of famine in Canaan. Going to Egypt had been a terrible mistake. "But we all have our 'Egypts,'" he muses, "those places and things to which we rush when the stress level rises. I learned early: find out what your 'Egypts' are and get rid of them."

Trust had come a bit easier to Abraham in the division of assets with Lot. "I was in the process of learning that maximizing my business profits was not the driver in my decisions. After the stupidity of having gone to Egypt, I wasn't going to Sodom. I'd trust God for whatever was best."

And that's why, many years later, when going up the mountain and having to respond to Isaac's question: "Where is the lamb?" Abraham would be able to say, "God Himself shall provide the lamb, my son." The smaller trusting incident back in Lot's time had laid the tracks for the greater trusting incident in Isaac's.

"I wasn't deceiving my son," he said. "Somehow I knew that when we reached the top, God would find a way to keep His promise to me. His purposes were hidden at the moment, but I had gone too far to turn back."

I tell Abraham of a book I've recently read by the late Henri Nouwen. In it he writes of his friendship with the Flying Rodleighs, a family of trapeze artists who perform in the circus. His associate, Sue Mosteller, writes of this relationship after Nouwen dies,

> He (Nouwen) saw in their performance the artistic realization of some of his deepest yearning, and he confesses that meeting them catapulted him into a new consciousness . . . Much of Henri's attraction to the trapeze performance had to do with the special relationships between the flyer and the catcher. The daredevil flyer swinging high above the crowd lets go of the trapeze to simply stretch out his arms and wait to feel the strong hands of the catcher pluck him out of the air. "The flyer must never catch the catcher," Rodleigh had once told him. "He must wait in absolute trust."

Abraham nods his head. "I understand that completely," he responds.

I imagine Abraham's eyes full of tears should he ever have sung with modern biblical people:

> Great is thy faithfulness, Great is thy faithfulness.
> Morning by morning new mercies I see.

All I have needed thy hand hath provided.
Great is thy faithfulness,
Lord, unto me.

Abraham raises the issue of generosity as part of the architecture of his converted life. He recounts the story of the strange appearance of Melchizedek, and how he sensed that the Voice of God was in this man. You know that you're experiencing transformation of life when something deep inside you *desires* to give in appreciation for all you've received.

"You gave a full 10 percent?" one of us asks.

"I gave Him a tenth of all I had."

Conversion had touched his wealth. And well that it had. Transformation of life would have been incomplete without this moment in Abraham's life. How could he have been prepared, if asked, to give his son's life on the altar at Moriah if he could not give a tenth of his material wealth? That puts a stop to the conversation for a moment as we all consider our holdings.

I marvel at this man who had grown up in a place where obedience, trust, and generosity were foreign concepts. But forty years later, hundreds if not thousands of miles later, difficult and challenging experiences later, here is a man of God: the father of all who believe.

"Man is like a tree," wrote Martin Buber.

If you stand in front of a tree and watch it incessantly to see how it grows and to see how much it has grown, you will see nothing at all. But tend to it at all times, prune the runners, and keep the vermin from it, and—all in good time—it will come into its growth. It is the same with man: all that is necessary is for him to overcome his obstacles, and he will thrive and grow. But it is not right to examine him every hour to see how much has been added to his growth.

As Abraham sits there and unfolds his tale of transformation, it becomes clearer and clearer: This man was a small tree that has grown into a mighty oak.

Finally, Abraham comes to the day the Voice of God Almighty called him to the mountain. He tells where he was at the very moment he heard the command. "No one would ever forget such an experience, such a place," he says.

You want to stop the man at this point. You want him to go slow and not leave out a detail. You wish you could get deep into his head and learn of every thought that swirled through his mind. Wasn't there any time when he wanted to protest? Didn't he go ballistic with anger? With doubt? With defiance?

But the old man shakes his head. And you hear him say, reminiscent of the words of Polycarp of Smyrna, who was asked if he would recant his faith in order to avoid execution, "Almost one hundred years have I walked through life in response to this Voice, God Most High, and He has never failed me. How could I withhold from Him now what He asks for, especially when it was always His (not mine) and His to command?"

Our conversation moves on. And then we hear Abraham move the subject away from himself and toward us.

"Let me remind you again. Someday *you* will be called to a mountain," Abraham says, breaking the silence. "You will be asked to bind up what is precious to you and give it back. And in that moment you will know whether or not you really ever *left*."

Are you as uncomfortable as I am? My mind reels with all that God has given: a wife and a marriage that stand on a strong platform of commitment and mercy. Two children of whom I am unashamedly proud. Five grandchildren who love me so much that they aren't yet sure that I have ever sinned. People who have permitted me into their lives as friends and students. Books I have been able to write, places I was permitted to visit, organizations I was allowed to lead. Health, a comfortable life, skills. What of this might God ask me (or you) to bring to the mountain?

As we leave Abraham and Sarah's table, thanking them for their hospitality, Abraham insists on walking us to the car. Father figure that he is, he slips his frail arm through mine so that he can draw me close and whisper into my ear.

I hear him say, "You know, they call me the father of all who believe. Do you know what that means to a man who had no children until he was one hundred? Why," and he chuckles as he says this, "we've had to give up sending birthday cards to them all. There are just too many. More than the stars of the sky, more than the sands of the sea."

And then Abraham whispers one more thing: "If you are fully transformed, you'll probably be a father to some who believe too."

As he says this, my mind snaps to another of Henri Nouwen's comments:

> I have always realized that I had little else to offer than my own, the journey I am making myself. How can I announce joy, peace, forgiveness and reconciliation unless they are part of my own flesh and blood? I have always wanted to be a good shepherd for others, but I have always known, too, that good shepherds lay down their lives— their pains and joys, their doubts and hopes, their fears and their love—for their friends.

As we drive away from the home of Abraham and Sarah, I hear myself praying deep in my inner being: *Oh, God, that You have adopted me into Your family is a remarkable act of grace. But I have miles to go before I will ever act fully like a family member. Increase the rate of my transformation, my mid-course corrections. Give me courage to accept Your hidden purposes. Whatever it takes, whatever it takes.*

LIFE'S MID-COURSE CORRECTIONS
Continue with the Challenge to Follow

By day the LORD went ahead of them in a pillar of cloud to guide them on their way and by night in a pillar of fire to give them light, so that they could travel by day or by night.

—EXODUS 13:21

After this, Jesus went out and saw a tax collector by the name of Levi sitting at his tax booth. "Follow me," Jesus said to him, and Levi got up, left everything and followed him.

—LUKE 5:27–28

Chapter 11

STOMPING BOOTS

My wife, Gail, and I had been in Hungary for a week building houses as part of a Habitat for Humanity team. Right on schedule the homes had been completed, dedicated, and turned over to their grateful owners. Now it was playtime, and that meant, in addition to sightseeing, a visit to one of Budapest's famous restaurants.

As expected, we enjoyed excellent Hungarian food. But what we hadn't anticipated was the lavish after-dinner entertainment in the form of folk dancing. As the tables were cleared, a stage (just a few feet from where we sat) suddenly was filled with a dozen or more dancers in peasant costumes. The women wore clothing of dazzling color. The men were all in black, and the things that most quickly caught the eye were their shiny, silver-studded, knee-length jackboots.

The dances began, and they were powerfully rhythmic. It was easy to forget whatever food was left on our plates and clap to the beat. The dancers, responding to our enthusiasm, became more and more fervent as they glided about the stage.

If the women in the dancing troupe had the job of dancing gracefully and effortlessly, the men had the responsibility for stomping out the beat with those boots of theirs. And they did it well, with class. The men found all sorts of creative ways to pound the stage floor (*phoom, phoom, phoom*) with those boots. It was very impressive for a while.

For me, a little folk dancing driven by relentless stomping can go a long way, and eventually, I was attracted to other things. To the musicians, for example, whose faces suggested a kind of professional boredom. To other tourists, mostly from Japan, who were mesmerized by it all. To the waiters carrying canisters of Hungarian wine that they flawlessly squirted from three or four feet away into the wineglass or the mouth of a risky (or tipsy) diner. But even those things hold one's attention for just so long.

Then I saw the bug. A beetle perhaps? No special brand; just your everyday generic bug-beetle: very black, lots of legs, quite ugly. He had come from somewhere underneath the stage and had begun to walk its edge from left to right. As he made his way, it was clear that he was oblivious to the dancers who were now wildly gyrating (and still stomping).

I quickly fixed on the bug (he was only feet away) and wondered if he had any idea of the show that was going on nearby. Did it occur to him that there might be significance to the seismic vibrations coming from the floor on which he walked? Surely, he must have felt them. Did his eye pick up any of the colorful, swirling skirts just above? Could he make any sense of the noise we call music? And what of the purpose behind his walk? Searching perhaps for leftovers from our meal?

Halfway across the front of the stage, the bug made a terrible decision. He made a left turn he never should have made. His new path took him right toward the stomping boots, a Bermuda Triangle, if ever there was one, for all bugs. Soon catastrophe was but feet away. The bug would be among those stomping boots, and only a miracle would avert a terrible moment.

As far as I know, no one else saw what was about to happen. The boots were furiously pounding up and down. *Phoom, phoom, phoom!* The dancing men in black were lined up like a human wall across the floor, their arms intertwined at shoulder level, their faces all turned uniformly to the right and then to the left. No one was looking down; no one cared about the tiny being headed in their direction. Bug and boots: They moved inexorably toward one another.

The first pair of boots to reach the vicinity of the bug struck the floor but missed by several inches, as did the second set. But the third didn't. There were just too many boots plunging downward to expect anything less than total disaster, bugwise.

When the third pair of boots had lifted back off the floor, there was nothing left. Not even a corpse. Only a tiny wet spot. And not long after that, even the spot was gone. I know this because I kept watching and thinking.

Think about how much this crazy little incident (which I have now told a score of times to audiences who think it quite funny) reflects upon life as we all know it. We are all "bugs," are we not, on history's stage. And every day we feel the seismic vibrations of those boots, the crushing events that are, if we are not careful, life threatening, career ending, health breaking, marriage and family dividing, spirit destroying.

Phoom, phoom, phoom the boots say. Throughout my life I've seen and heard them. I saw the stomping boots in a hailstorm that wiped out the farmers in Kansas I once served as a young pastor. I've seen them in the downsizing announcements that cost the jobs of men and women I've known and loved. The boots appear in the words spoken by a physician who brings the bad news of cancer to a patient. The boots are present in the horror created by the drunk driver who crosses the center line and crashes into a family car, taking the life of a young father and husband.

The stomping boots are the armies that rape and pillage, the economies that seem to favor the fortunes of the rich and add to the further miseries of the poor. The boots are stomping when a young man filled with the zeal to become someone feels the subtle resistance of another who hates his ethnic identity, when parents watch a son or daughter they dearly love slip into the clutches of a druggish peer culture that cares nothing about the future. The boots are coming down when we discover we've been swindled, polluted, and deceived.

Even as I write these words, we are watching the people of western Turkey dig out from a devastating earthquake. In a way that defies imagination, the boots have stomped down on one city after another, leaving thousands dead and many more thousands trapped and injured in buildings and homes that have totally collapsed. And each of us wonders when we might find ourselves among our own version of the stomping boots.

It is among those boots that we find out who we are and what we might become. The key word is *character*. As a term, *character* does not identify us by our physical appearance, our influence in the community, our education, or our wealth. Character is not about the cars we drive, the achievements we ring up, or the charm and charisma we manifest. Character is who we are at soul-level, the hidden life within us, and how we are most likely to think and act both in the routines of the day and in life's toughest moments when the boots begin to stomp.

As I think about the people I have known, I find myself sorting them into a series of simple categories. There are those who are skilled or talented in some extraordinary way. Then there are those who are remarkably brilliant or whose minds are muscular and seminal. I can think of some who are always a lot of laughs, the source of much fun. There are also the powerful and dominating, the successful, the clever, the creative, and the persuasive (they've got a great plan for your life).

On the darker side, I've met those whose lives are driven by anger and resentment, those who are captive to obsessions and compulsions, those who are selfish and egotistical, and those who are exploitative and make you feel used.

But above and beyond all these, there is a special category that I save for a relatively few number of people I've known. People of character.

And when I review this group and ask why I have matched them up to this word, I realize it's because each of them has faced an assortment of stomping boot moments and demonstrated a response or an initiative that can be described only with words such as *noble, brave, wise,* and *selfless.* The biblical writers liked the word *godly.* When in their presence, you are aware that something deep within you leaps with respect and deep admiration. Their very being calls you to a higher way of thinking and of behaving. You want to be like them.

I'm thinking of the man who downsizes his public life or leadership to care for his wife whose mind is gone. The couple who could have terminated the pregnancy of a severely deformed child but choose to take it to term and welcome the child into their family as a gift from God. The man I know who will not descend to the lowered levels of his critics to fight them. And the woman who chooses the moral high ground and, as a result, loses out on the possibility of a marriage. The physician who steps away from a career that offers high income to run a clinic in a developing nation.

In each of these cases, a defining moment or choice identifies them as people of character, but when you get close, you usually discover that the extraordinary thing they've done is merely a reflection of the way they live the rest of their lives, whether you're around to see or not. They do not do what they do nor is their demeanor shaped in order to gather the admiration and praise of others. This is simply who they are as people and would be even if they were stranded alone on a desert island.

Few people in the history of the American Christian movement have more to teach us than John Woolman, a Quaker businessman who lived in colonial America during the mid-1700s. His journal fairly oozes with comments that are character-based. Here are a few random comments, to illustrate character, the life of the hidden person, as Woolman saw it. I have included them along with their misspellings and strange capitalizations as they come directly from his journal.

- In the management of my outward affairs, I may say with thankfulness I found Truth to be my Support.

- My mind through the power of Truth was in a good degree weaned from the desire of outward greatness, and I was learning to be content with real conveniences that were not costly; so that a way of life free from much Entanglements, appeared best for me, though the income was small.

- [On visiting a congregation] the Lord I believe hath a people in those parts who are honestly concerned to Serve him, But many I fear are too much clogged with the things of this life, and do not come forward bearing the cross in such faithfulness as the Almighty calls for.

- [On sensing the presence of God in the middle of the night] As I lay still without any surprise . . . words are spoken to my inward ear which filled my whole inward man.

- [Reflecting on a meeting where he felt constrained to remain silent] I found no Engagement to Speak . . . and there fore kept Silence, finding by Experience that to keep pace with the gentle Motions of Truth, and never move but as That Opens the way, is necessary for the true Servant of Christ.

This remarkable man, Woolman, brought enormous influence to his generation regarding the evils of excessive wealth and the holding of slaves. His was one of the first prophetic voices to speak out against the wickedness of the slave trade. If you want to study the relationship of the hidden person to outer morality and righteousness, you can do no better than to read the life of John Woolman.

Many of us reach the point at midlife where we take a hard look at our personal architecture of character and are a bit disappointed at what we see. We feel that we are a bit frayed about the edges. We see the tendency to stretch the truth if it will impress others, the hints of jealousy toward younger men and women who have an energy of enthusiasm and vision that we once had, the instinctive reluctance to challenge words or behaviors that are unjust or short of biblical standards.

We grow alarmed at irritabilities, envies, lusts, and resentments we thought we had once overcome but now appear to have lurked somewhere within waiting for us to let our guard down.

And when we see ourselves in the small and large stomping boot moments and do not like what we see, we cry out. Am I changeable? Is character formed in early life malleable enough that it can be reshaped?

Abraham was kind enough to introduce us to the first kind of change. The change in faith, when we must reorient our belief system and *leave* what has shaped us in the past for something new. This second kind of change, the change in character, speaks to who we are and who we are becoming.

Once again we could pore through the biblical material and find person after person who could inform us on character issues. Abraham's nephew, Lot, could tell us much about how (maybe why) his personal architecture of character fell below the line of acceptability when he made choices that led him to the lower plain of Sodom. Saul, first king of Israel, had all the surface markings of a leader when he took over responsibility for Israel's fortunes. But it was soon clear that he was more interested in being a celebrity than a man of character. Interestingly enough, his son Jonathan was quite the opposite.

The prophet Hosea showed character as he chose not to be vindictive when his philandering wife left him a second time. The character of John the Baptizer was quite obvious when he launched thunderous words of prophetic contempt upon a local king with the morals of an alley cat. Biblical examples of character and noncharacter abound.

Character is the hidden life of the person. It is formed slowly over a lifetime. The qualities of character are revealed most powerfully in the stomping boots moments when, under great pressure, we draw from the depths whatever courage and wisdom are to be found there. These same qualities are evidenced over the long haul when we line up the dots of a person's everyday conduct and conversation in the routines of life.

I want to take a look at two communities of people who can teach us something about character. The first group, the wandering congregation of Israel, has something to instruct us about shabby, unacceptable character. Theirs is an interesting but sad story. The second group, the disciples of our Lord, offers us a lesson in how character is reformed.

Many are fond of saying that the great character battles are fought in our youngest years. Perhaps. But I've wondered about the character battles of the middle years when there is a temptation to grow lax in the maintenance of the hidden life.

In his middle years, for example, David the king suddenly showed a collapse of character in his sin with Bathsheba. What could have prevented it? Answer: greater attention to the hidden life.

George Macdonald (no relation) once wrote,

Foolish is the man, and there are many such men, who would rid himself of his feelings of discomfort by setting the world right, by waging war on the evils around him, while he neglects that integral part of the world where lies his business, his first business—namely, his own character and conduct.

Two centuries ago John Quincy Adams wrote to his daughter about the standards she should set in selecting a husband. "Regard the honor and moral character of the man, more than all other circumstances, think of no other greatness but that of the soul, no other riches but those of the heart." Adams had his finger on the hidden life.

The operative word is *follow* and keep on *following*. It's the only safe way to make it through the stomping boots.

Chapter 12

GROWING DOWN

In the movie *Shine*, we are introduced to David Helfgott, the Australian musical genius whose young life was crushed under the oppression and abuse of a highly possessive father. When his mind could no longer accept the strain, it unraveled, and Helfgott was institutionalized for years. Later, at a better time in life, he said, "I guess I didn't grow up; I grew down." A rather graphic phrase that could be used to describe a spiritual journey.

When Abraham left the mountaintop having heard the words, "Now I know that you fear God," it would be tempting to think that the generations succeeding this righteous man would perpetuate his life of acquired faith. His high point on the mountain could have been their spiritual baseline. But that's not the way things happened. In fact, using Helfgott's words, Abraham's descendants seem to have grown down. Some exceptional moments in succeeding generations? Yes, but not many.

It cannot be said that Isaac was a man of signal character, nor is there much in which to take delight concerning *his* (Isaac's) sons, Jacob and Esau. Jacob, the younger, whom God mysteriously elects (against all ancient tradition) to be the primary player in the family

125

line, consistently shows remarkably poor judgment. By nature, he is a liar and conniver and reflects the Abraham of the earlier days who played with the truth to protect himself.

The best that one might say of Jacob, in my opinion, is "Thank God he's in the biblical family line; with him there, we don't look so bad." Jacob mellowed as he grew older, and his more kindly demeanor in later years offers hope to us. Even though his behavior is strange on sporadic occasions, the Jacob the Bible gives us in his later years suggests that the man came around. He changed. His character seems to have matured.

But, oh, his sons. Who of them would you have liked as a friend? These are the men who, in a jealous rage against Joseph, their younger brother, sold him off as a slave to a caravan headed for Egypt and lied about it to their father.

Out of all these brothers, it would appear that only Joseph gathers to himself some of the characteristics that we believe were grafted into the life of Abraham. Joseph, whose superior character would reveal itself in the stomping boots moment of sexual temptation, in his conduct while in prison, in his ability to offer leadership to a beleaguered Egyptian government administration when bribes and corruption could have run rampant. Put Joseph on the A-list when it comes to architecture of character.

But in the long run, we are watching a family line grow down. The people who had been given the stamp of "chosen," the family of Abraham, are not an admirable lot.

Not long after Joseph's death, the descendants of Abraham were pressed into slavery by the Egyptians. An entire tribe of people forced into a life that, ironically, would take them backward to a world not that different from the one their forefather, Abraham, had lived in before he left Ur. Although he was not enslaved physically and economically as they were, Abraham was enslaved to a way of thought that was not that far different from what Israel experienced.

And that's the way it would be for the family of Abraham for four hundred years—captivity, increasingly harsh treatment, total demoralization. Time enough for a collective mind-set to lose every ounce of vital optimism, hope, that had been generated in Abraham's lifetime. *The family of Abraham grew down!*

Approximately sixteen to twenty generations later, the Voice spoke out of a burning bush in the desert to a man whose name was Moses. He was eighty at the time, a few years older than we imagine Abraham to be when he heard the word *leave*. This time the operative word would be *follow,* and the leader chosen by God would be Moses.

If it took Abraham thirty to forty years to acquire the disciplines of obedience, trust, and stewardship so that he could model true faith on the mountain, it took Moses eighty years to acquire the listening ear that would permit him to understand God's hidden purposes.

Moses' task was not only to extricate the people from Egypt. That was a relatively simple matter. Moses' real day job was to teach Israel (as God had taught Abraham) a new way of thinking, a unique way of living, a special brand of vital optimism.

Novelist Herman Wouk describes Moses' task well:

Economists know that, contrary to the popular impression, slaves do not work hard. A slave civilization is slow-moving and easy going . . . Take away a man's rights in himself, and he becomes dull and sluggish, wily and evasive, a master of the arts of avoiding responsibility and expending little energy. The whip is no answer to this universal human reaction. There is no answer to it. The lash stings a slave who has halted dumbly, out of indifference and inertia, into resuming the slothful pace of his fellow slaves. It can do no more. The slave's life is a dog's life, degraded, but not wearying, and—for a broken spirit—not unpleasant . . .

Vital faith would be a long time in coming to Israel. The great lawgiver, Moses, inherited a generation of Hebrews that had descended from 400 years of slavery. The powerful trust in God which their ancestor Abraham had learned to generate was hardly a memory now. *400 years of slavery had virtually eliminated all the good spiritual genes. Moses would have to start over.* (Emphasis mine)

Wouk underscores that the ways of life and thought learned in Egypt will not be rubbed out easily. Israel's character (what little good can be said of it) has been ravaged. It hardly exists. It will have to be rebuilt. Wouk writes,

The generation of Jews that Moses led into the desert collapsed into despair and panic over and over in moments of crisis. Broken by slavery, they could not shake free of improvidence, cowardice, and idol-worship. All the men who had been slaves in Egypt had to die in the desert, and a new generation had to take up their arms and their religion, before the Jews could cross the Jordan.

If there is to be transformation of character, if the hidden life of Israel is to be reborn, it will happen as they travel through the stomping boots of their time. The adversaries and the circumstances they'll face will surface all the ugliness that has been stored up in their collective hearts. Habits, unhealthy traditions, acquired appetites and passions will be identified and judged, sometimes with terrible harshness. But it will take that to get Israel's attention.

In the wilderness Israel will have to unlearn ways of thought unacceptable to their God. Their instincts of defiance and rebellion against leadership, their knee-jerk tendency to quit, to run backward in the face of struggle, their proneness to absorb the ways and convictions of any society near them will be exposed as evidence of the vacuousness of their hidden life.

God said to Israel through Moses, "Although the whole earth is mine, you will be for me a kingdom of priests and a holy nation" (Ex. 19:5–6).

Given the apparent absence of any kind of admirable character in these people who are to follow Moses, this seems about as absurd a statement as the one Abraham heard when he was told that he would be the father of a great nation. If Abraham struggled to believe, what kind of a problem did Moses have as he contemplated the proclivities of the people?

It would take a long time to see even the slightest hint of character reformation in Israel. And that's why I find the stories of the Hebrews in the desert important. They show me, first, what life with marginal character looks like. There is a humbling dimension to these stories, for as I read them I see myself, my natural tendencies. Like Israel, I am "on the road," and their need for rebuilding character is also mine.

A pastor friend told his congregation one morning, "If you knew everything about me that God knows, you'd never come to this church. But if I knew everything about *you* that God knows, I wouldn't let you in this church." After the laughter subsided, we all thought about the truthfulness behind the comment. And it was sobering.

Watch these people in action with their dearth of character. Like me, you will quickly learn what we need to include in our prayers of repentance. Their ability or willingness to follow is tragically short-lived. So it is with most of us.

The Voice that called Abraham has spoken to Moses. When asked, "What is [your] name?" God answers, "I AM WHO I AM" (Ex. 3:13–14).

Today we refer to this name as YHWH (some have used the name Jehovah). Thomas Cahill is helpful in noting that there are at least three ways to interpret the name given to Moses out of the bush: It can express the nature of God as Creator, or the greatness of God as One who is absolutely incomprehensible to the human being, or the promise of God that He will be constantly present to His people. All three introduce a God who is above all gods—God Almighty, God Most High, the Father of Abraham.

When the great liberation from Egypt happened, it became the responsibility of Israel to follow. In their commitment to follow would come the formation of their character as the people of God: "By day the LORD went ahead of them in a pillar of cloud to guide them on their way and by night in a pillar of fire to give them light, so that they could travel by day or night" (Ex. 13:21).

WELCOME TO THE WILDERNESS
Discouragement: My Character Is Dysfunctional

Moses and the Hebrew people had just said a bitter farewell to Egypt. The moment of liberation was behind them, and it was time to get on with their journey to the promised land. The God of Moses had provided an incredible show of force, one you would think that both friend and enemy would never forget.

There may have been a short time of euphoria, but the quality of Israel's character faced a test almost immediately. Soon after exiting Egypt proper, they arrived on the shores of the Red Sea, no insignificant obstacle. About that time someone looked backward and saw the Egyptian army in pursuit. Pharaoh had apparently changed his mind and wished the Hebrews back. Given the circumstances, there was an instant collapse of courage:

> They were terrified and cried out to the LORD. They said to Moses, "Was it because there were no graves in Egypt that you brought us to the desert to die? What have you done to us by bringing us out of Egypt? Didn't we say to you in Egypt, 'Leave us alone; let us serve the Egyptians'? It would have been better for us to serve the Egyptians than to die in the desert!" (Ex. 14:10–12)

Moses was the model of coolness under fire. His own character, sharpened in the wilderness over a period of forty years, rising toward vital optimism, shone here diamondlike: "Moses answered the people, 'Do not be afraid. Stand firm and you will see the deliverance the LORD will bring you today. The Egyptians you see today you will never see again. The LORD will fight for you; you need only to be still'" (Ex. 14:13–14).

And that's exactly what happened. Before long the Israelites were through the parted waters, and the pursuing Egyptians were drowning in them. It was a marvelous moment (if you were a Hebrew), and it prompted an interruption in their journey for the purposes of thanksgiving. Wise decision. The song of Moses and Miriam (Ex. 15) is an expression of joy and gratitude that Israel had for God that day. From total discouragement to one of the greatest moments of praise in the entire Bible: that's quite a trip over a day or two.

I think of how often I have had similar moments. Perhaps not as dramatic as watching water back up and then witnessing the destruction of a division of crack army troops. But my moments have been dramatic enough for me. Moments when my back was to the wall, and there seemed no way out. A total lack of guidance necessary for a decision, or resources needed to see a project through; watching someone you love very much going through a trial.

You do what you've been taught all your life: go to your knees (all night if necessary). You pray with abandon, pour your heart out to God. You make lots of promises. And you witness what can only be called a miracle. Something happens to convince you that God has, indeed, acted. It is an incredible moment.

So it must have been for Israel. I understand the joy.

What I do not understand (in them or in me) is how quickly the song of Exodus 15 can be forgotten, how fast discouragement can return. For not long after the Red Sea drama, Israel was out in the wilderness, and the people had a new problem: the issue of food.

In the desert the whole community grumbled against Moses and Aaron. The Israelites said to them, "If only we had died by the LORD's hand in Egypt! There we sat around pots of meat and ate all the food we wanted, but you have brought us out into this desert to starve this entire assembly to death" (Ex. 16:3–4).

Discouraged people rewrote history. Minds were distorted. Yesterday's blessings were forgotten. No longer remembered was the slave-life of Egypt; in fact, it sounded as if life back there was one perpetual party. Overlooked was their deliverance at the Red Sea. Suddenly, Moses was the bad guy, and Egypt's Pharaoh actually looked better every day. Talk about revisionism.

This is how the mind works when someone questions the adequacy of God. And it is not exclusively ancient thinking. Rather, it is as contemporary as can be. It describes the mind-set of we moderns who are tempted to panic every time we face a Red Sea or wilderness experience.

Lucretius the Roman philosopher wrote: "Look at a man in the midst of doubt and danger, and you will learn in his hour of adversity what he really is. It is then that true utterances are wrung from the recesses of his breast. The mask is torn off; the reality remains."

The nagging, troubling question is, Why was Israel's collective memory so short? Could not a God who could beat Pharaoh into submission, who could separate waters, who could crush an army manage a relatively small matter such as food? Why does Israel forget so quickly? (And why, O Lord, have I so often done the same?) This shortsightedness: It's the stuff that kills vital optimism. And it happens to those who do not daily monitor the quality of their faith.

It is a moment for a learning experience. For character building. God said, "I will rain down bread from heaven for you. The people are to go out each day and gather enough for that day. In this way I will test them and see whether they will *follow* my instructions" (Ex. 16:4, emphasis mine).

And Israel learned. As Abraham had learned to trust God for a son, so Israel learned how to trust God for daily bread. How to rest on the Sabbath. How not to hoard and attempt to amass wealth on the back of God's blessings.

"Take a jar and put an omer of manna [bread] in it. Then place it before the LORD to be kept for the generations to come," the Lord told Moses (Ex. 16:33). The development of the hidden life requires reminders and the upgrading of memory. We would like to think that this was enough learning. But, of course, it wasn't.

AT THE FOOT OF THE MOUNTAIN
Disconnection: My Character Slips Easily Out of Touch with God

Characterlessness is in evidence when I carry on with the gestures of religion but have no sensation of connection with the One who is the object of my worship.

- "I have no sense of God's presence at all in my world."

- "For me, praying is like talking to a stone."

- "I get rattled, even angry, every time someone says, 'I felt the Lord saying to me . . .'"

I have heard these things said, and in earlier days I probably said them too. I have a feeling that this is what the Hebrews were saying as they waited impatiently for Moses at the bottom of Mount Sinai. After getting past those initial "hiccups" in the first days of their journey, the Hebrews had moved south in the Sinai desert until they were before the great mountain. Moses had been to the top and back in conversation with God.

But this time he stayed at the summit longer than they thought he should. And they had a community case of the jitters. What little faith they had quickly began to dissipate; they felt disjointed and vulnerable.

Finally, they concluded that their leader wasn't coming down from that mountain. And in a short time the quality of Israel's character was once again in shambles.

The solution? A conference with Aaron, the brother of Moses who was supposedly in charge of the general spiritual life of the community: "Come, make us gods who will go before us. As for this fellow Moses who brought us up out of Egypt, we don't know what has happened to him" (Ex. 32:1). I have always found it amazing that Aaron listened to this proposal and bent to it.

What went wrong? In Israel's case they had to connect with "something" they could see. For four hundred years they'd lived in an Egypt full of idolatrous worship. It had gotten into their bloodstream.

As long as Moses was with them, they could rely on Moses' God. But take Moses off the scene for too long, and their "faith" (at least what little there was) went south. Is it clear that Moses' God was not yet Israel's God? No Moses, no God.

Just that quickly, they were prepared to forget the great show of force at Exodus time and get back to life as they'd known it. Soon they were dancing around a golden calf. Scholars suggest that more than dancing was going on. Without a doubt all the old sexual frenzy of such pagan rituals was present; drunkenness prevailed. Sacrificial rites were employed that spoke deeply with familiarity into everything these people and their ancestors had known while in Egypt. It was as if they had totally forgotten everything good and godly.

When Moses came off the mountain, he found his people engaged in this full-scale orgy of pagan worship. "It is the sound of singing that I hear," he told Joshua, his traveling companion (Ex. 32:18). And when they came close enough to see for themselves, they found the *children of God* dancing up a storm. Moses' anger could not have been more inflamed.

When asked about the golden calf, Aaron seems to have shrugged his shoulders and said, "They gave me the gold, and I threw it into the fire, and out came this calf!" (Ex. 32:24). You want to say, "Yeah, right!"

I have known this story all the days of my life. I have laughed at the impatience and the stupidity of the people at the bottom of the mountain. I have been perplexed by the shallowness of Aaron's leadership and his subsequent denial of responsibility. And I have resonated with Moses' anger as he came off the mountain and saw this spectacle.

But as I have grown older and have come to grasp how foolish can be the thinking and the actions of people in a moment of disconnection, I think I understand this story a bit better.

In an old book on my shelves, I read C. H. Macintosh, who wrote, "There is a crisis in every man's history, at which it will assuredly be made manifest on what ground he is resting, by what motives he is actuated, and by what objects he is animated."

The Israelites certainly told on themselves that day when Moses came off the mountain. Feeling disconnected, the people created something, anything, to assuage their anxieties. And it was a strong indicator of insufficient character. It is enough to say at this point that wherever people feel that their character is not grounded in God, a golden calf will become necessary.

To people of my generation, dancing around a golden calf seems rather ridiculous. It occurs to me that *our* golden calves may take the forms of cars more elaborate than we need, homes larger than we need, and gadgets in greater proliferation than we need. I have come to recognize occasional times when a need arises in me to buy something. Not something that I necessarily need. But there is a desire to acquire, to *have* something that will make me feel good for a while.

A faster computer (although the speed of my computer has not sped up my writing), a sportier car, a better stereo system. I don't have to spend big bucks; I just get these "hankerings" occasionally for something new. And this impulse is frequently indicative of the same sort of thing going on at the foot of Sinai. The spiritual jitters, disconnectedness. One needs something to dance around.

It is relatively easy to choose not to purchase whatever has suddenly seemed attractive. But what may be more important is to search the soul to ask why the impulse to build a golden calf has surfaced.

FALSE START
Doubt: My Character Rests on Slippery Ground

In the months that followed those moments at the mountain where Israel first heard God's law and principles of life, they journeyed among the stomping boots of the wilderness. Here and there were battles fought and most won due to demonstrations of God's assisting power. Chapter after chapter tells the stories of the faithfulness of God, and you want to believe that all of this is accumulating in the memory bank of the people. Sooner or later they will get it as Abraham finally got it. Jehovah is a trustworthy God. To follow Him is to realize the fruits of faith.

But then there is a place called Kadesh Barnea, entrance to the promised land. Twelve spies were sent into the land of Canaan (Abraham's old stomping grounds) to check on details such as the people, the cities and fortifications, the quality of soil, the agriculture.

When they returned, the spies had a majority and a minority report. Ten claimed that entering Canaan would be disastrous. Two others, Joshua and Caleb—men with unquenchable vital optimism—suggested that they get started on invasion plans immediately. The people chose to hear this:

"We can't attack those people; they are stronger than we are." And they spread among the Israelites a bad report about the land they had explored. They said, "The land we explored devours those living in it. All the people we saw there are of great size . . . We seemed like grasshoppers in our own eyes, and we looked the same to them." (Num. 13:31–33)

What did the people do? They "raised their voices and wept aloud" (Num. 14:1). And the majority report prevailed.

Put simply, the people of Israel decided that the God who had rescued them from Egypt, sustained them in the early stages of the wilderness trek with food and water, and empowered them in battle had missed this one. He had given bad directions. And they were afraid.

Fear and doubt are cousins. Children fear; adults doubt. It's the same thing. Both erode faith. It leads to the lukewarmness spoken of in other parts of Scripture and eventuates in disappointment. Few things are more deadly in organized religion than to talk about the great acts of the God of the Bible as history, yet deny their possibility in the present. This gap of disbelief destroys all possibility of vital optimism.

I cannot read the story of the people of Israel standing there at the edge of the promised land without wondering about my own reaction had I been one of the decision makers. I want to see myself lining up with Joshua and Caleb. I fear the possibility that the other ten might have been more persuasive.

And so the boots stomp down again and again. And each time they do they reveal one more empty spot in the hidden life of the people God has chosen for Himself. They follow, but pathetically so. *Dragged* might be a better word. Still they are on the way, with many more lessons to learn.

I find it easier to be charitable toward Israel if I remember a day in my own spiritual journey when I fell into a bitter cauldron of doubt. I had become convinced that I knew God's purposes for my life. But when circumstances did not point in that direction, in fact pointed in the opposite direction, I found the situation unacceptable.

My perception (I could not fight the temptation to think differently) was that God had made a fool of me. He had led me to my own Kadesh Barnea and now appeared to leave me there twisting, as they say, in the wind. That was the day I understood how the people of Israel felt. Betrayed! More than once I prefaced what prayers I offered with the words, "God, I no longer understand Your language."

In both cases, Israel's and mine, our character showed itself in great disarray. It took some time for me to rebound from that experience. And now, many years later, I have no doubt that God knew what He was about: His purposes were hidden from me, and I needed to learn how to trust.

The people of Israel stand paralyzed at Kadesh Barnea. Their mid-course correction is in serious trouble. They are growing down.

Chapter 13

GROWING FURTHER DOWN

For forty years the people of God, the children of Abraham, trekked back and forth across the expansive wilderness that bordered the promised land. Again and again they felt the cruelty of the stomping boots. But rarely could it be said that they were growing up in the hidden life. In truth, they seemed to be growing down.

Recalling these ancient narratives of Israel's journey through the wilderness is an unsettling and searching spiritual exercise for me. They are certainly not new or strange stories. I remember hearing the stories told over and over again when I was a child.

At the time, Israel's life in the wilderness (like Abraham's life on the road) was, more or less, just a collection of adventure stories I liked to read. But, as we say, children are good observers but poor interpreters. I'm afraid I didn't get it; I didn't see far enough to understand the soul behind these dysfunctional behaviors. It was only as an adult, after a few stomping boot experiences of my own, that I saw these stories in a new light.

I saw Israel in me! Their collective behavior as a people in each stomping boot episode revealed to me more and more of the default human condition when biblical character is missing. Four hundred years of slavery had indeed grown a people down. How long would it take to grow them up where they might begin to reflect the reputation of their spiritual father, Abraham?

Let me repeat myself. Among the values in knowing these stories, gaining as intimate a view of them as we can, is the guide they offer to the confessional dimension of our spiritual journey. If all we do in our meditations is to repent of a few petty acts called sins that have accumulated over the last day (and this is not to belittle the importance of doing that), we have not known the deep power of purifying grace that repentance is supposed to offer. Israel and its stories help me to understand the deep underlying currents of evil response and intent, the tragic aquifers far beneath my conscious life that will continually feed my daily life with impurity unless they are identified and replaced with alternatives of the kind of character God built into Abraham.

In this bleak but necessary recitation of Israel's diminutive character, let us wander on to Midian.

BEWARE YOUR NEIGHBORS
Drift: My Character Is Eroding Away

The puzzling story of Israel when it arrives in the region of Midian the land of the Moabites does not make for pleasant reading. There is a huge buildup and then a quick and dirty conclusion. But the lesson encased in the whole of the episode is startling and deserves attention.

Who were the Moabites? In the earlier story of Abraham and Lot, we read that while he was in a drunken condition, the daughters of Lot seduced him. The older daughter conceived a child on that occasion who became "the father of the Moabites." Centuries later we learn the rest of the story.

The key player in the region of Midian was the king of Moab,

Balak son of Zippor, who was well aware that wherever the Hebrews had previously been, there was trouble for the locals. Balak knew that it was just a matter of time before conflict would break out in his own backyard.

That knowledge moved him to establish contact with a notorious seer, Balaam, son of Beor (try not to confuse the names). With Balaam's magical powers of cursing and blessing, Balak reasoned, the inevitable fight with Abraham's descendants could be swung in his favor. The boss was prepared, Balak's reps said to Balaam, to pay big bucks for an effective curse that would neutralize Moses and his people. Balak admitted: "They are too powerful for me. Perhaps then [given a good stiff curse] I will be able to defeat them and drive them out of the country. For I know that those you bless are blessed, and those you curse are cursed" (Num. 22:6).

After a night of thinking through the deal, Balaam refused. He had heard the Voice of God telling him to stay out of the arrangement. Thus, the next morning Balak's people headed home. But soon they were back, and their second offer was apparently one that Balaam found hard to refuse. Soon he was on his way to launch the curse and collect the fee.

That trip features the rather amusing story of Balaam and his talking donkey. The older biblical translations referred to Balaam's transportation as an ass. More than once in my childhood, I and my friends were booted from Sunday school because we could not halt our snickering over such an unchurchy word as *ass*. My teachers had no sense of humor about it. New Bible translations have laundered the word, changing it to *donkey,* and have thus saved countless children from exiting Sunday school prematurely.

If you know the story, you may recall that an angel of the Lord stood in the narrow roadway, but only the donkey was perceptive enough to see him. When the donkey turned aside into a field, Balaam beat her harshly. The second time the donkey saw the angel, she

141

brushed a wall and injured Balaam's foot. The third time, the donkey
simply lay down, and Balaam lost his self-control.

The storyteller said, "Then the LORD opened the donkey's mouth"
(Num. 22:28).

"What have I done to you to make you beat me these three times?"
There follows a discussion between the man and the donkey in which
the donkey is clearly the more reasonable, the more perceptive.

"Have I been in the habit of doing this to you?" the donkey asked
Balaam.

And Balaam actually answered, no.

It's a great story! "Then the LORD opened Balaam's eyes, and he
saw the angel of the LORD standing in the road with his sword drawn.
So he bowed low and fell facedown"(Num. 22:31).

When the angel finished with Balaam, he was a convinced man. No
cursing of Israel. Subsequently, Balaam went to Balak and offered a reality check. His comments can be summed up in this brief exchange:

> The LORD their God is with them [Israel];
>> the shout of the King is among them.
> God brought them out of Egypt;
>> they have the strength of a wild ox. (Num. 23:21–22)

That says it all. As one might expect, Balaam was fired, sent home
without an honorarium. "And Balak went his own way" (Num. 24:25).

But that is not the conclusion of the story. All of that was merely
a setup for the lesson in Israel's corporate character. The next paragraphs are an unpleasant read. In fact, I can see how the story might
offend modern senses. But we must always read these stories with the
question in mind: *What is the writer trying to say out of his times?* We
not only want to know the story, but we seek, most of all, to discern
what universal message the story is sending.

Here is Israel in a most embarrassing moment:

> While Israel was staying in Shittim [Balak's country], the men began to indulge in sexual immorality with Moabite women, who invited them to the sacrifices to their gods. The people ate and bowed down before these gods. So Israel joined in worshiping the Baal of Peor. And the LORD's anger burned against them. (Num. 25:1–3)

Before going a step further, remember the story of Balaam. In that strange tale God set the stage for a sure victory. Balak, the king, was neutralized. *All Israel had to do was to live in accordance with the miraculous provision of safety that had been made for them.*

And this is where the issue of character enters. Did the people of Israel have it in their hearts to live up to the gift that had been given them? Answer: no.

It was not military strength that stopped Israel. It was, once again, the people's ineffectual character. What Balak's armies could never have done, Moab's women accomplished handily. Israel's men couldn't say no. Their sexual appetites prevailed.

Their forefather, Abraham, had been commanded to *leave* all of this. His descendants had, in effect, gone back to the very beginning. This would have been a great moment for a lecture from their ancestor Joseph who might have suggested to them his own character battle in the home of Potiphar.

The immediate response to this problem of fraternization with the enemy was a rather violent one. And it is here that many of us would wish that the story might end, that we could disassociate ourselves from the biblical narrative. God's initial response to this mess was almost savage. Moses was instructed to eliminate by execution the leaders who were responsible for Israel's infidelity. We may want to recoil at the severity of the decree from heaven. But keep an eye on the underlying message.

The message has to do with character—individual and corporate.

To *follow* means to submit to a scrubbing of the soul, something that cannot happen in a day. Generations of accumulated habits and attitudes had to be purged from the people. They have lived in a world where their decisions were made for them. A world in which they had little practice in making discriminating and prudent choices. They might have been physically strong enough to win military battles, but they were pathetic at soul-level. Put a moral temptation in front of them, and they were, as we say, "toast."

Building in the hidden life of the people would not be done easily. Make a nation out of them in a generation or so? Possibly. But a corporate character? A culture that *followed* after the God who once spoke to Abraham? That would take some time.

For a moment the story worsens. The writer focused upon an individual Hebrew and his Moabite girlfriend who apparently epitomized everything that had gone wrong. Unfortunately for them, they happened to be headed for the man's home just as Moses and his leadership team were meeting to discuss the problem. Poor timing!

One of Moses' men, Phinehas, saw them. Aroused to blazing anger, he followed them to their home and killed them on the spot. Although his summary action does not suit our times, it was clear that his action ameliorated God's anger. Why?

I can only assume that God saw in Phinehas a spark of the character He was hoping would soon reside in the rest. Here was a man who had suddenly come to understand the horror of a community *or a person* without character. For Phinehas, it was a moment to eradicate habits and actions poisoning the soul. His anger, in that context, was a sign of something of a mid-course correction. Phinehas was following.

It has been very difficult for me to relate this story that seems so crude. I would have preferred to have excised it from my writing. Someone could argue that it is the kind of episode that zealots and bigots seize to justify their hatred and their violence against anyone they deem to be "impure."

Is there a place for the anger of a Phinehas? Obviously, his actions would be intolerable in our day. I hope that we have appropriate disciplinary systems today that can deal with such sin. But the more important message is that of the hatred of sin and the understanding that when evil is tolerated in the character of a community or just one person, everyone suffers. Israel had to learn that what happened in Midian was conduct unbecoming a child of Abraham.

JERICHO IS A MINEFIELD
Denial: My Faith Is Riddled with Secrets

The fight for the architecture of Israel's character continued. As in Abraham's Mother-may-I life, there were bright spots and more than a few dark spots. The character-building lessons abounded all along the way.

If I were to pick one or two more that have instructed me, I would bounce some years ahead to a time when Israel crossed the Jordan into the promised land under the leadership of Moses' successor, Joshua.

The city of Jericho stood at the entrance to the land. It would have to be defeated if Israel was to move farther.

Again, the story we heard as children of the walls of Jericho kept us in wonder. We heard of their extraordinary width and impenetrability. We heard of Jericho's strong defense and of the consternation of Israel's people who still, after all of God's provision, had about as little self-starting courage as one can imagine.

The strategy, said the Lord, would be one of marching, not battle. For six days, the people marched in silence around the city once each day. And on the seventh, they made the trip seven times. At an arranged signal the people began to shout, the horns of the priests were blown, and the walls of the city were shattered. A confident city, trusting in its walls, fell quickly to the Hebrews.

Here is where the next character lesson began. "Keep away from the devoted things," Joshua had told his people,

> so that you will not bring about your own destruction by taking any of them. Otherwise you will make the camp of Israel liable to destruction and bring trouble on it. All the silver and gold and the articles of bronze and iron are sacred to the LORD and must go into his treasury. (Josh. 6:18–19)

The "devoted things" refers to things said to belong to God because they were declared to be His. Isaac, lying bound on an altar, was in effect a devoted thing or, better said, a devoted person. He belonged to the Lord. A tithe given to Melchizedek was a devoted amount of money.

Somewhere in the planning process or by command given to him, Joshua had declared that certain kinds of treasures found in the city were not to be taken as booty. They were *devoted things*. They were consecrated to God.

At the Battle of Jericho, Israel's character would be tested by keeping its hands off the devoted things: the silver and gold and bronze found in the city. In Midian, the men were supposed to keep their hands away from the Midianite women. They had not. In Jericho, they were to keep their hands off the silver and gold and bronze. Would they?

As far as we know, all but one person complied.

Achan, son of Carmi, son of Zimri, son of Zerah, of the tribe of Judah, had a different idea. He secreted some of the devoted things in the floor of his tent. And he had every reason, at first, to think that he had gotten away with it.

Achan lived in a time when people thought that gods had relatively limited knowledge or willpower. Bury something (as Achan had done) or go away some distance (as Jonah tried to do) or smooth things over (as David and Bathsheba attempted with sacrifices), and you might get away with your secret. It was bad theology.

Again, this is one of those stories we heard scores of times in childhood. It helped form the aspect of our faith that said God cannot be fooled. And yet all of us tried and keep trying. We were (and are) wrong. Biblically defined character is based on the working knowledge that nothing can be hidden from God.

The character lesson *du jour* came to a head when, unexpectedly, things started to go downhill for the Israelites. A small band of overconfident soldiers was humiliated in a skirmish at a tiny village called Ai. It was a wake-up call for Joshua, a signal that something was amiss. Listen to his anguish:

> Joshua tore his clothes and fell facedown to the ground before the ark of the LORD, remaining there till evening. The elders of Israel did the same, and sprinkled dust on their heads. And Joshua said, "Ah, Sovereign LORD, why did you ever bring this people across the Jordan to deliver us into the hands of the Amorites to destroy us? If only we had been content to stay on the other side of the Jordan! O Lord, what can I say, now that Israel has been routed by its enemies? The Canaanites and the other people of the country will hear about this and they will surround us and wipe out our name from the earth. What then will you do for your own great name?" (Josh. 7:6–9)

God's answer to Joshua was blunt. Israel had sinned: "That is why the Israelites cannot stand against their enemies . . . I will not be with you anymore unless you destroy whatever among you is devoted to destruction . . . You cannot stand against your enemies until you remove it" (Josh 7:12–13).

As I have studied this story at the age of sixty, I am once again impressed with how differently I respond from when I was a six-year-old. Then it was just an adventure story. Today it is an awesome reminder of how my sense of character has been formed. For the story reminds me that a man is only as solid (characterwise) as the most secretive things in his life.

When I was a child, I was far too naïve to appreciate the significance of this dimension of character. I grew up in both a family and a church where it seemed that the only way to survive was to keep secrets. Don't tell your parents where you were or how you really feel. Keep your real thoughts to yourself; honesty about your doubts or your fears or your temptations in the life of the church will be paid off in gossip and criticism. You will not be loved or valued.

As I have known each of Israel's character failures, I have also known Achan's failure. I know all too well the life of the secret carrier who hides a portion of his life under the tent, hoping that no one, perhaps not even God, will notice. And to the extent that any one of us does this, character takes a beating.

It is difficult once again to read that Israel must obliterate Aachan and his family from the life of the community. The ancients would have understood the desire of the community to rid itself of all potential carriers of Aachan character disposition. If biblical character was ever to have a chance to grow, the spirit of this family—secret carrying—would have to be flushed.

IT SOUNDS LIKE A BAD ENDING
Defiance: My Faith Is Gone

The long view of Israel's character development is not good. Would that one could point to a succeeding generation after all this fuss and say, Here is a community of people whose corporate character does, indeed, reflect the image of their God. But that was never to be so.

It might be reasonable to ask, Why did God stick with these people? Answer: He loved them, and He had made a promise to their father, Abraham. God is not a promise-breaker. His character is holy.

But He did discipline them. Severely!

When Joshua dispersed the people into the various sectors of the promised land, the character of most people again went "south." The minute they were out of range of their spiritual leader, the news was not good.

> After Joshua had dismissed the Israelites, they went to take possession of the land, each to his own inheritance. The people served the LORD throughout the lifetime of Joshua and of the elders who outlived him and who had seen all the great things the LORD had done for Israel . . .
>
> Joshua . . . died at the age of a hundred and ten . . . And they buried him . . .
>
> After that whole generation had been gathered to their fathers, another generation grew up, who knew neither the LORD nor what he had done for Israel. Then the Israelites did evil in the eyes of the LORD and served the Baals. They forsook the LORD, the God of their fathers, who had brought them out of Egypt. They followed and worshiped various gods of the peoples around them. They provoked the LORD to anger . . . In his anger against Israel the LORD handed them over to raiders who plundered them. (Judg. 2:6–14)

The character of the people of God seemed to grow increasingly ugly. The biblical writer finally wrote of this gloomy period of Israel's history: "In those days Israel had no king; everyone did as he saw fit" (Judg. 17:6). They kept growing down. Life among the stomping boots did not necessarily raise a nobility of spirit; it revealed a paucity of spirit.

The story of Israel's character had disclosed discouragement, disappointment, drift, denial, and now outright defiance. Without powerful, forceful men of character like Moses and Joshua, Israel was nothing. As Lot was nothing without Abraham, Israel was nothing without its two great leaders. In effect, the character and faith of two men over a period of 125 years had kept the people together. And now that they were gone, there was little else but defiance and ultimate disintegration.

For the most part the history of Israel hardly differed from this pattern for a thousand years until Jesus came. Now and then a remarkable person of biblical character emerged in response to the pleas of desperation that people would raise heavenward. God would provide a Gideon or a Deborah to step to the front for a few short years. When there were prophets, the character of the nation might climb a notch or two, but usually for a short time. A few kings dared to lead the people to higher ground. But in truth the character of the people remained largely shallow, buoyed up only by the remarkable qualities of a few people, the so-called faithful remnant.

In truth, Israel refused to follow with any level of consistency. Had it done so, the God who had led Abraham would have led the people to remarkable heights.

What can the downward spiral of Israel's history teach me more than three thousand years later? Israel has touched virtually all the bases that require ongoing repentance and humility in the modern life. Left to ourselves, we tend to head in Israel's direction; we replicate the behaviors. Only a regular, disciplined determination to engage in the surrendered life of following will keep us from the wrong kind of mid-course correction.

Fortunately, there is a better story in Israel's future. For One will come who is the visible representation of the Voice that called to our father, Abraham. And those who follow Him will grow great character. The hidden life will flower.

Chapter 14

Is There an "Israel" in Me?

The stories of Israel that I have related in the last two chapters have left me shaken. I have known them all my life—at least I thought I knew them—but now in my older years as I write about them, they enter my hidden life with a brand-new force.

No longer do I read them as biblical adventure. Rather, I read them in a more personal way. I am constrained with alarming frequency (and with deepening humility) to say, "I am Israel. I see myself among the people. I, too, am as capable of growing *down* as I am of growing *up*."

It would appear that there was little, if any, natural nobility in Israel's life. Which is to say that when left to themselves on any given day, the people chose the darker alternative in any stomping boot moment. Rarely did they ascend to higher ground. Complaining, running after alternative gods, sulking in despair, scapegoating whenever possible—these seem to be a rough profile of Israel's disposition in the wilderness and, later, in the promised land. This is their default character, *the way they are* unless called to a superior level of life.

Which is what often happened and what rescued them from catastrophe. Again and again God raised up men and women who would gain Israel's attention for a moment. And if the people followed after them, imminent disasters were reversed. But there came a time when God no longer raised such people up, and Israel ran out of gas. There followed a terrible era of humiliation and chastisement. I can think of only one reason why they ever survived. *God loved them;* He had promised Abraham that they would endure.

Am I really Israel? Am I too hard on myself? Or does the truth best lie in the assertion that *there is an Israel in me?*

Henri Nouwen, in the last year before he died, mused in his journal on a morning after seeing the opera *Carmen.* He had been moved by the way Carmen, the wily, spirited Gypsy woman, had managed to gain the affections of Don José, the quintessential Spanish soldier who is committed to obeying his commanding officer and living his life strictly by the book. When both the temptress and the tempted are destroyed, Nouwen observed, "I do not know what would happen if a Carmen barged into my life and swept me off my feet." For all of his lifetime of seeking after God, Nouwen understood the deeper parts of himself, the restlessness, the defiant spirit lurking like a dangerous animal.

Not understanding this, Israel never met a "Carmen" it didn't fall for. It lacked the internal disposition to believe God for the longer haul, the hidden purposes that He had first begun to reveal to Abraham.

Israel failed to appreciate the unexplored territory of the hidden life. It didn't occur to the people that there was a long-term purpose in something such as a portable sanctuary being situated in the center of their wandering community. In that most holy place, the priests would intercede for the people, make right the sins of the community, remember the mighty acts of salvation that God had initiated on their behalf.

Those were visible, corporate events; in part, their purpose was to help people understand that the disciplines should be mirrored in the hidden life of every individual. The life of the soul, the hidden place, must be taken seriously. Building up the outer world in one's life was necessary; building up the inner world was indispensable. God yearned that Israel, both as community and as individuals, might look instinctively to Him for direction.

All the way through our years, we will battle to acquire an intimacy with God. Rarely will the enlargement of the hidden life come close to matching the competing demands of the visible life. When we are young, we will be tempted to think that we are too busy establishing our identity and our place in the pecking order of things. When we are older, we will tend to fall for the notion that it's too late to change.

Is the total alteration of the hidden life too much of a challenge? Is Israel evidence that it can't be done? Is it possible that the occasional person of unusual biblical character, then and now, is more of an anomaly than anything else?

I would be tempted to offer a far more gloomy answer to these questions if it were not for a second set of stories. For another community within the community of Abraham's people ascended to a higher level of biblical character. Not easily, not quickly, not without setbacks. But they demonstrated what can happen *if* following is taken seriously.

Centuries and centuries after Israel had wilted in the wilderness among the stomping boots of its time, the apostle Paul would write of an alternative life: "We, who with unveiled faces all reflect the Lord's glory, are being transformed into his likeness with ever-increasing glory, which comes from the Lord, who is the Spirit" (2 Cor. 3:18). With a vital optimism that came from his conversion to Christ, Paul saw the marvelous scheme of life-change, the remaking of the hidden life through the power of the Cross.

Let me make the wild assertion in order to establish my point that most of us in the modern biblical movement have missed this, not deliberately, but because we have our minds on too many other things. We are a people out to convert the world before we have converted ourselves. Not that we should wait for the one until the other has happened. But it is possible that we might do our converting work a bit more humbly and a bit more effectively if we attended to our own conversions first.

"Work out your salvation with fear and trembling," wrote Paul as he urged a group of Christ-followers to attend to their hidden lives with great seriousness (Phil. 2:12).

There is a sense in which the history of the Older Testament is a sad story. It does not end well. We watch a nation of people whom God loves systematically spurn all of His efforts to call them to Himself. Finally, the patience of God ran out.

Then a most interesting thing happened. The Voice spoke once again as it spoke to Abraham. But the Voice came among the people. The Voice was the Word incarnate. "He came unto His own," the writer John declared, "and He lived among us full of grace and truth."

And why was He here? To show forth faith in its most perfect form. To call people to follow Him into biblically defined character. To set in motion a movement of people who would perpetuate that character for all the future. His command: follow! To Abraham, the word was *leave*. To another people in another time, the Voice said, *Follow!* And those who followed Him changed!

Chapter 15

THE MANY DOLLS

Recent visitors to our home from the country of Moldova gave us a Russian doll in appreciation of our hospitality. The doll stands about nine inches high, is made of wood, and is beautifully painted with bright colors. It is shaped like a duckpin, the kind you'd see in a bowling alley.

The head of this doll can be twisted off. And when it is removed, you discover tightly tucked inside, another doll, a replica of the first, only slightly smaller. And if you remove this second head, you find a third doll, which in turn contains a fourth, which contains a fifth, and so on until you have six dolls, the smallest less than two inches tall.

The Russian doll sat for some time on my desk as a memento of an enjoyable visit. And then one day in a pensive moment I reached for it and began to separate out all six progressively smaller versions of the doll until they stood before me looking like a family of sextuplets.

These dolls are a representation of a complex human system named Gordon, I found myself thinking. Perhaps they are one Gordon in six parts, or perhaps they are six Gordons in one. You could say that there's a Gordon within a Gordon within a Gordon within a Gordon, six selves. I wonder if the first and the largest Gordon even knows the fifth Gordon?

If this doesn't make a whole lot of sense, that's okay because it's what I call streaming (stream-of-consciousness thinking).

There are Gordons within me that never see the light of day, but on occasion, they demand to be heard. They instigate thoughts and propose behaviors that can be shocking to other parts of me.

There may be Gordons in the group of "me" who may not even like or agree with other Gordons in the group. Perhaps there is one Gordon who is a rebel in the opinion of all the others. And perhaps there is a Gordon who listens keenly to God but who is resisted by the others. Could it be that there are occasions when one Gordon actually betrays another? Maybe there's a Gordon or two in this mix who are not at all in alignment with the purposes of God. In fact resistant? All of these Gordons are part of the neighborhood of my hidden life.

I have brought the Russian doll to a number of gatherings where I have been asked to give talks. Each time I've explained what I've just written. And as I have introduced each of the dolls, I have put them on a table in disorder, isolated, scattered from one another, suggesting that this is their most natural formation. Sometimes I have used one doll to violently knock over another and send it spinning as a picture of how conflicted we can actually be. What many begin to visualize as they see the multiple of similarly appearing dolls is the internal discord that often plagues each of us.

I have also suggested that the audience imagine a second doll with five other selves. The second doll may be a spouse, a parent, a child, an associate at work. Now we have seven selves connecting with six other selves. And who knows what levels of dissonance that will engender? No wonder satisfying community of any kind is so elusive.

When evil invaded the human condition, the result was a stunning disconnection not only among people but within oneself. Put simply, our "me" became many dissident selves who fell out of rapport with one another. From that time forward each of us has been not one but many with attitudes and motives and purposes that are rarely in alignment. And this is our problem: We may think that we have our many selves under control, but that may not be the case. Just when I think I present myself as an integrated, fully aligned person to my immediate world, I discover that there is a part of me independently functioning like a small child who is always running from his mother.

A man possessed of demons came toward Jesus. "What is your name?" Jesus asked.

"My name is Legion," he replied "for *we* are many" (Mark 5:9, emphasis mine). It sounds as if the many dolls (some of them strangers) spoke for the outer doll. Who knows which ones belonged there and which ones did not?

I have met people who, although not demon possessed in my judgment, have nevertheless reflected this inner civil war. "Everyone has his own theater," Julius and Augustus Hare write, "in which he is manager, actor, prompter, playwright, sceneshifter, [ticket seller], doorkeeper, all in one, and audience into the bargain."

I begin to understand what Paul was saying when he wrote, "I do not understand what I do. For what I want to do I do not do, but what I hate I do" (Rom. 7:15). A Russian doll might have helped him illustrate his point.

I visit with a stunningly handsome man in his early sixties who has starred for many years in several television soap operas. He is an alumnus of several marriages, a drinker-out-of-control, incapable (so he says) of any moral decisiveness, uncontrollably restless, full of fears.

"Tell me who you are in two minutes," I say to him.

"I couldn't do that if you gave me an hour," he answers. "I've played so many roles and characters in my years in the entertainment business that I no longer know which one I am. The real *me* got lost in the shuffle a long time ago."

Even as he speaks it occurs to me that I've seen what he is saying when I have visited with other men and women (not all, of course) in the world of the theater. They have become so adept at assuming one role after another that they have lost track of which one they actually are. And so it becomes easy to assume a convenient role to fit whatever the moment calls for.

This disconnection obviously presents a problem. Who are we anyway? Do we know? Who's really in charge of me *if* there is within my hidden person a gang of Mafia-like characters who will stop at nothing to assert themselves? Which am I when I stand before a group of people to give a talk on the subject of biblical community and the importance of loving and serving one another? Am I the Gordon who speaks with passion? Or am I the Gordon who, suddenly noting a person in the audience who has been a consistent critic, feels a rush of resentment and hostility? Am I the man who believes in unconditional, grace-driven relationships or the man who really harbors anger toward another? And am I other men at the same time?

Perhaps more important than the question, Who am I? is the question, Who is it that our Maker wishes me to be? That leads us to the issue of the *architecture of character,* a phrase that describes as well as any I can find the underlying essence of who we are and how that is evidenced in the thoughts we think, the words we speak, and the actions we take. Character speaks to how well my many selves are in accord, on the same page, speaking the same language.

We have just taken a look at Israel on its journey. The architecture of the national character has been poor. It has not stood up to the demands of stomping boot moments. Like a poorly designed building that collapses in a hurricane or an earthquake, Israel has not met the grade.

In his *Letters and Papers from Prison,* Dietrich Bonhoeffer, one of WWII's great Christian martyrs, frets that people of character, those who draw from the hidden life, may be in too short supply:

We have been silent witnesses of evil deeds; we have been drenched
by many storms; we have learnt the arts of equivocation and pre-

tence; experience has made us suspicious of others and kept us from being truthful and open; intolerable conflicts have worn us down and even made us cynical. Are we still of any use? What we shall need is not geniuses, or cynics, or misanthropes, or clever tacticians, *but plain, honest, straightforward men*. Will our inward power of resistance be strong enough, and our honesty with ourselves remorseless enough, for us to find our way back to simplicity and straightforwardness? (Emphasis mine)

Bonhoeffer knew what character looked like for him. We must be clear about what biblical character looks like for us. For even thieves have a definition of character. And I would suppose there was even a concept of character that the Nazis, Bonhoeffer's adversaries, recognized. At the risk of repetition, let us be plain: We are not talking about the production of nice people, of men and women who make no waves, cause their world no trouble. We are speaking, rather, of people who are defined by the character of Jesus Christ. They project an appealing mystery in their overall demeanor. Having been with them, we feel as if we know Jesus better.

When Jesus entered the world in human form, He came in part to rebuild humanity to conform with the image of the Creator. It would necessitate a reconciliation between God and His people. It would result in further reconciliation among many selves (dolls) within us. And it would provide the impetus and the power to create reconciliation between people and the formation of a divine community.

And what is required to make this happen? *To follow.*

For more than a millennium a group of people, first a family and then a nation, had worked the character problem. Here and there had been individuals, sets of people, who showed all the fruits of biblically defined character. Like Abraham, they had learned to hear His Voice and obey. They, too, had trusted, and they, too, understood that life was a stewardship in which they were called to live as a holy nation, a kingdom of priests. But the efforts of a few were often clouded by the defiance of the many:

> The LORD, the God of their fathers, sent word to them through his messengers again and again, because he had pity on his people and on his dwelling place. But they mocked God's messengers, despised his words and scoffed at his prophets until the wrath of the LORD was aroused against his people and there was no remedy. (2 Chron. 36:15–16)

Into this historical morass of stomping boots, where innocent people were being crushed with horrific regularity, came the Voice incarnate. His name was Jesus, and He would say, "I am the way and the truth and the life" (John 14:6). His message could be reduced to a few simple words: repent (*leave*), follow, and I will make you into something new. Enlarging upon those ideas, He would employ phrases such as being *born again*. Jesus was in the business of reinventing people.

If Moses stepped forward to raise up a nation, Jesus raised up a band of people that never seems to have numbered more than a few hundred. And of the hundreds, we can vouch for only a few dozen men and women who, in the space of three years, went through a character transplant of immense proportions.

When we seek samples of character rebuilding, it would be hard not to focus on Simon Peter about whom, I suppose, we have more information (both good and bad) than any of the others around Jesus. We have Levi, also called Matthew, who, we can assume, came from a business environment known for its greed and corruption. Simon the Zealot, who on former occasions would have loved to have pulled a man like Matthew into a dark alley in order to disembowel him, is a transformed one.

James, Andrew, and John are fishermen from a tough part of the world and seem to evidence rather volatile tempers when crossed. Finally, there is Thomas, who may or may not be as tough as the others, but has a major problem with skepticism and doubt.

The women around Jesus are a unique lot. One or two of them appear to have come from very dark pasts and must have had stories of their own when it came to a descent into the multilayers of evil. Some seem to have been women of means who had family connections that may have provided funding for the nomadic life the disciples occasionally lived.

All of them, both men and women, are transformed, changed. Their characters are brought—not instantly but processively—into alignment with the mind and Spirit of Christ. *And before they die, they will have prepared the way for the changing of the known world.*

How was that done?

Just as it was done with Abraham.

We do not have a record of each occasion, but it is safe to say that each heard a version of the invitation: *follow me.*

Nowhere can I find in the four Gospels any instance of our modern version of evangelism. No one was asked to pray a prayer and then told that he was "in." No one was asked to affirm a set of doctrines or propositions. All were judged on one simple basis: Were they following Jesus or not?

It is clear that following spoke of the direction one was walking in. In this case only two directions were possible. Either you were walking *toward* Him (no matter the distance from you to Him), or you were walking *away* from Him.

Anthropologists have pointed out that various cultures define *alignment* in two different ways. Imagine a circle that is defined by its outer circumference. In this scheme one is either in or out of the circle. And those inside the circle define what it will take for those outside to get in.

This, I'm afraid, is not much different from the modern concept of organization that most of us have known in the past few hundred years, business or religious. We want to know the boundary line and what it takes to get in.

The second alternative for alignment is not concerned about the circumference of the circle and who is in or out. Rather, the important matter is what (or who) is at the center. In this case, the question, in contrast to who is in and who is out, becomes, *Are you moving toward the center or away from it?*

The words of our Lord—to follow—make sense only when we understand that Jesus defined *relationship* in terms of the second of these alternatives.

When the disciples came to Him upset because they had met a man who was casting demons out of people, they said, "We told him to stop, because he wasn't one of us [circle]." But Jesus said, "Don't stop him; he who is not against me is for me [center point]."

The start of character transformation is movement toward the center point of Christ. There is little, if anything, in the concept of a circle that compels people to deepen in character. Once they are over the line and inside the circle, what does it profit to be concerned about the hidden life any longer?

But if Jesus is the center point, and He bids us come closer and closer, then there is incentive each day to reengage in increasing transformation. The closer we move to the center, the more like the One at the center we become. Moving closer—deliberately, strategically— becomes one's personal mission over the course of a lifetime.

If I have belabored this point beyond the line of tolerability, it is because I feel as if I'm dealing with a fundamental misunderstanding in our perception of what it means to be biblical people. For too many of us, transformation consists of altering some behaviors, some vocabulary, some schedules, even some priorities. And we rejoice all too quickly when these alterations appear to happen. But the hidden life is far more important. If the heart remains untouched, as seems to have been Israel's problem, then the possibilities of genuine mid-course correction are diminished.

In a brief but interesting episode in the New Testament book of Acts, a man known as Simon was "converted" under the evangelistic efforts of Philip. Simon had been a man of immense local influence as a magician. He had enjoyed much popularity, and of him it was said, "This man is the divine power known as the Great Power" (Acts 8:10).

When Philip entered his world, Simon saw that whatever power he had was much less in magnitude than Philip's. Therefore, "Simon himself believed and was baptized. And he followed Philip every-where, astonished by the great signs and miracles he saw" (Acts 8:13).

The indication is that Simon changed. It would also seem that he was initially welcomed into the community of believing people. It was only when two apostles, Peter and John, came for a visit that Simon's true colors became obvious.

Impressed with the apparently even greater powers possessed by the apostles, Simon offered to pay them *if* they would "franchise" out to him the use of these powers. Peter hit the ceiling:

> May your money perish with you, because you thought you could buy the gift of God with money! You have no part or share in this ministry, because your heart is not right before God. Repent of this wickedness and pray to the Lord. Perhaps he will forgive you for having such a thought in your heart. For I see that you are full of bitterness and captive to sin. (Acts 8:20–23)

One is left to speculate on whether Simon had actually been con-verted into faith. I leave the judgment to others. But my point is that Peter saw *into* Simon's hidden life at deeper levels and recognized the conflicted "dolls" within this man. The man had miles to go before character was transformed.

So how is the hidden life transformed? In *Doctor Faustus,*

Thomas Mann puts the question this way: "There is at bottom only one problem in the world . . . How does one break through? How does one get into the open? How does one burst the cocoon and become a butterfly?"

The answer came along with Jesus Christ. His power to overcome the inertia of Israel and find a handful of men and women who were ready to surrender their hidden lives to Him and let themselves undergo mid-course correction is stunning.

Chrysostom said it rather well, I think: "To be another than I am I must abandon that I am."

And that's where it began for a group of very common men when Jesus came. They discovered life-change to the very bottom of their hidden lives.

Chapter 16

WHAT FOLLOWING LOOKS LIKE

I have had the privilege of knowing many men and women of extraordinary character in the years of my life. But one man stands out among them all. His name was Marvin Goldberg. I write "was" because he died not long ago.

I met Marvin Goldberg when I left my Colorado home to attend the Stony Brook School on Long Island, New York. Soon after I arrived, he went to work on my hidden life.

I was fifteen years old. My recollection was that I was small, physically puny, socially immature, and academically mediocre. My fantasy was to be a prep school football player, a star running back. But the dream was not so mercifully put to death during the first week of fall practice. It became abundantly clear that I lacked the required nerve as well as the pounds to carry a football up the middle and into the line. I was fast, however.

My first conversation with Goldberg was in conjunction with the Stony Brook track-and-field program, which he directed as head coach.

"I'd like you to come down to the field tomorrow and work out with a few of the track men," he said. "I think we might make a runner out of you."

The next day I appeared in shorts and sneakers and ran a few wind sprints for him. He made a few encouraging comments about my running style and suggested I come back again the next day. I did, and I kept coming each day after that. There was something about Marvin Goldberg that made you want to be near him. You knew instantly that he would bring the best out of you, that he would care for you in ways that far exceeded the world of the quarter-mile oval. Something deep within said, "Stick with this man, and you're going to grow." Even as a fifteen-year-old I was perceptive enough to get that message.

In a few weeks, Coach Goldberg had me working out as a potential member of the relay team that would compete at the annual Penn Relays in Philadelphia. He spent hours teaching me how to burst out of the starting blocks, how to bring my body up slowly from the starting crouch to full running position. I learned how to pump my arms, to lengthen my stride, to relax the muscles of my neck and face so that I would not cut off my wind. Members of the team were taught how to hand off the relay baton in full stride inside the "box" in accordance with the rules of relay racing. Goldberg was a perfectionist about these things and showed us movies of teams that had lost close races because a hand off was muffed or because stride was broken.

Each day there would be carefully designed and individualized workouts to strengthen the body and bring stamina to the heart and lungs. The Englishman Roger Bannister had just broken the four-minute-mile barrier and had presented the runner's world an entirely new understanding of athletic conditioning. The fact was, Bannister demonstrated, the athlete had a much greater capacity for development than anyone had ever thought. Coach Goldberg agreed with that assessment, and he proceeded to push us harder than any Stony Brook athletes had been pushed before. "The practices during the week will be painful at times," he told us, "but you'll come to learn that the race on Saturday will be a pleasure."

Although I came to the track team as something of a sprinter, Coach Goldberg soon had me running on his cross-country team (five miles). "It will build your endurance," he said, "and it will be good for the battle you face in your mind." The coach knew that, in the end, a large part of competition on the track is psychological.

Each afternoon we came to the track and checked a bulletin board that displayed each runner's workout plan for the day. Most of us dreaded this moment as we read the coach's latest menu for "suffering." As we read the schedule written in his distinct handwriting, we would silently protest, "There's no way I can do this." And then we would go out and do it for him! He was tough, but we trusted that if he said we could do it, we would be able to do it.

Coach Goldberg was not only committed to developing runners. He made no secret of the fact that he had a passion for building men (Stony Brook was at that time a boys' school). Every bit of an athletic experience, as far as the coach was concerned, was tied tightly to some aspect of character development. He believed in the hidden life and in its deliberate cultivation. And he made it happen in the context of our athletic world.

In my first competitive experience, I was entered in the 200-meter. There were six runners including me on the starting line, but it was clear that my most serious challenge would come from a runner named Alverez who wore the uniform of the Trinity Pawling School. He was big, seemed a bit overweight, walked about heavily. As I pounded the spikes that would hold my starting blocks in place, I actually dared to say to Coach Goldberg, "I don't think I'll have any trouble taking him."

Soon we were crouched in our blocks. The starter barked the traditional commands ("Runners, on your marks . . ."), and the gun sounded. All six runners shot up and out of their starting positions and down the straightaway. About twenty-two seconds later Alverez won going away.

As I walked dejectedly back along the track, Coach Goldberg joined me. "Gordie [I was Gordie in those days and remain that today *only* to my wife], I have something to say to you. When you told me that you would have no trouble beating Alverez, I knew you had lost the race already. And I decided to let you lose it even though it might hurt the overall team scoring.

"Gordie, you must never, ever underestimate a competitor on the basis of what he looks like or what you've heard about him. First of all, you judged him on the basis of his body and not on the basis of his heart. Until you know what's in a man, you'll never know what the man is.

"Second, you must *never* measure yourself against a competitor; you measure only against yourself. And this is the way it will be all the way through life. If your eyes are on what you think your competitors are going to do and not on the best you yourself can do, you'll lose all kinds of races over and over again."

I never underestimated a competitor on the track ever again. And as hard as it was, I learned from moments like these in the company of Marvin Goldberg never to match myself—intellectually, professionally, spiritually—against anyone else in my adult life. The coach was laying the tracks for the day when it would become clear to me as a biblical person that all of life is played for an audience of One and never as a competition against my peers.

Many races later, I found myself one day at the starting line of the 400 meters. Once again the coach was there with me. The name of the runner to beat was Carlin. "Now, Gordie, I'd like you to come off the blocks in total relaxation. Get up on Carlin's shoulder and stay there. Stay there! Don't try going around him until you're coming off the last turn. Then kick with all you've got. Carlin has superior speed, but you have conditioning. Your race—and I want this to be your race—is in your kick, and you can do your best if you'll trust in the stamina you've built up. You'll have *more* in the last forty yards because we've trained you to have more. So wait until the end and kick! You don't want to get into a serious sprint with Carlin or anyone else in the first three-fourths of the race. Wait for the last turn, remember! Now go do your best."

The race began, and as I'd been told, I came up to Carlin's shoulder. But as I rounded the *first* turn, I made a decision to depart from the plan. Carlin didn't seem to be running as fast as I'd anticipated. It would be nice, I thought, to lead this race all the way. I remember thinking about the girlfriend at trackside who had come to see me compete. She would be impressed, I thought. Thus, to get her attention as much as anything, I blew past Carlin as we moved up the backstretch.

It was a serious mistake. No sooner had I cleared him than he exploded and passed me as if I were standing still. I never caught Carlin, and he won by ten yards.

"Gordie, I think we need to think about what happened here," Coach Goldberg was saying minutes later. "Did you not hear my instructions, or did you simply choose to ignore them when you started running?"

"Sir, I'm afraid I chose to do things my own way." The tradition of Stony Brookers was to address their seniors as "sir" or "ma'am."

"I'm not half as concerned about the fact that a race was lost as I am about the habit pattern I see in you. You do not listen well. And this problem is going to mark your entire life. It is beginning to look to me as if you will have to learn all the important lessons of life the hard way instead of learning from those who can point the way for you. I wonder how many more races you'll have to lose before you master these things? And I wonder how many mistakes you'll make in life until you figure this out?"

The coach's rebuke was more painful than his workouts. I had let him down terribly. How long, I wondered, would he put up with a foolish athlete who took up a lot of his valuable time all week in practice and then failed him in the race? I left the track that day vowing

169

that I would stop learning lessons, if possible, the hard way. I have worked at this ever since. Marvin Goldberg was the first person to make me aware of this serious flaw in my hidden life in a way that I could see it clearly.

In another of my books I recounted the day when I ran the first leg for our mile relay team at the Penn Relays. Our team had been assigned the second lane. Starting in the first lane was the team from Poly Prep in Brooklyn. Their leadoff runner was a well-known sprinter who held a conference record for the 100-yard dash.

I have told the story elsewhere of his greeting when we shook hands prior to getting into our starting blocks. "May the best man win," he said. "I'll be waiting for you at the finish line."

Batons in hand, the eight runners took off at the sound of the starter's gun. Within twenty-five yards the runner from Poly Prep had disappeared around the first turn. In my mind I began to settle early for second place on my leg of the relay. And then, about three hundred yards into the race, I saw the runner from Poly Prep just ahead, barely jogging. The seven of us flashed past him as if he were standing still. I like to finish the story with a grin and slyly say, "In kindness I waited for the man from Poly Prep at the finish line."

But that is not the end of the story. Coach Goldberg was also at the finish line. He wanted to talk as soon as the race was over. And when the fourth runner on our team had crossed the line some three minutes later, the two of us, coach and athlete, walked the infield grass together. All about were dozens of other runners warming up for their races, and surrounding us in the stadium were forty thousand noisy spectators. Marvin Goldberg was oblivious to all of them.

"Gordie, I heard what he said to you before the race started. And I want you to remember all your life what happened. The man could easily have beaten you or anyone else if the race had been only 220 yards. But the race was 440 yards long, and he wasn't prepared for that distance. You were. He had speed, but you had stamina.

"And that's going to be the lesson of life. Learn the difference between speed and stamina, and don't confuse the two. What good is a man who can run fast but can't finish the race? Always run to finish, Gordie, always run to finish . . . and to finish strong." As he said this, the coach put his hand on my shoulder and looked me straight in the eye. Looking back, I believe he sensed the greatest challenge I would have in my architecture of character. And he was using the story of a race to build what he hoped would be a better man.

One more Goldberg story.

In the first year that I began to run competitively, the coach invited me to his home for dinner. His wife, Dorothy, prepared a lovely meal, ate with us, cleared the table, and then left the room.

Marvin Goldberg reached out for a school notebook on the table behind him. I could see that on the cover he had written my name. What was this book about me, and why would a man go to all the trouble to put it together? He opened it to the last page and placed it where my plate had been. At the top of the page was written "June 1957," a date three years and three months from that evening.

"Gordie, study this plan with me."

I saw the names of several track meets that are annually scheduled during the month of June. Listed under each track meet were events in which I might be entered. The 220 meters, the 400, and possibly, the 800. And with each race there was a finishing time: the seconds or minutes and seconds that it might take for me to run that particular event. They were light-years, it seemed to me, ahead of the times I was running. Not only that, I saw that in each successive meet in June of 1957, the times continued to improve. In the final scheduled races of the month, the times were absolutely mind-boggling.

"This is the kind of track man I think you can become over the next three years. It's what I expect your running to look like three years and three months from now."

The standard he was setting for me went beyond what any runner in the history of the school achieved in those events. Clearly, he wanted to make me into one of the best athletes the school had ever had.

Then the coach turned the pages backward. And as we moved from back to front, I could see that each page corresponded to a month of the year. Thirty-nine pages: thirty-nine months back to where we were right now. On each page were lists of races and workouts, times becoming faster and faster until they reached the level of what I'd seen for June 1957. I could see that he had poured hours into creating a long-range plan of development. He knew where I was *now*, and he knew where he wanted me to be *then*.

"Sir, do you really think . . ."

"Trust me; this is you three years from now."

And then he went on.

"Now, Gordie, I want you to know that this is about much more than running times. It's about becoming a man. There are other goals far more important than these running times to think about. I'm going to push you to be a leader, to be faithful to your commitments, to keep up on academic discipline, to encourage younger runners, to grow in your Christian life. I am going to be tough on you, and there will be days when you simply won't like me. But if you'll stick with me, this is what you'll become."

I stuck with him and the plan. I *followed*. Not that faithfully always, but I followed.

Things did not always go smoothly. Two years later there came a time when, for a strange summer moment, I wanted to quit. I had enough medals; I was weary of workouts. I was tired of giving up my weekends for competition; I was sick of keeping all the disciplines.

From my Colorado home, I wrote to Coach Goldberg and told him that when I returned to school in the fall, I was going to enjoy myself a little more. "It's my last year," I wrote, "and I'd like to have some fun." Track? Maybe in the spring. But the long-distance competitions of the fall cross-country schedule? Not this time.

I was abandoning the plan. In actuality I was reverting to an alarming trait in my character: quitting.

Strangely, it didn't occur to me that Marvin Goldberg would have an opinion on my decision. "If you'll stick with me . . . ," he had said.

His response came in the form of a six-page letter. Reduced to a simple point, the letter said, "Your decision to quit may be one of the most important decisions you'll ever make. For if you decide to leave the team because you do not like hard work and because you want to enjoy yourself, you will reinforce a habit pattern that will cause you to quit the next time things are tough. You'll find it easy to forget commitments you've made to other people. You'll always wonder what might have happened if you'd given it your best. I want you to reconsider and return to the team even if you do not like the pain and the disciplines. I promise you, if you do, you'll look back a hundred times during the rest of your life and be thankful you did."

I returned to the team. And, yes, I resented some of the hard work, although I loved the victories. As the year wore on, I reached most of the goals that Coach Goldberg had put down in that notebook three years earlier. And today, forty-plus years later, I never tackle a challenge (including the writing of this book) without saying somewhere along the line, "I did it then; I can do it now."

That's what happens in the hidden life when one follows. And Marvin Goldberg was worth following.

Chapter 17

HEARING THE VOICE

Many years ago I had the privilege of meeting a remarkable Christian philosopher, Emile Cailliet. Cailliet spent much of his life as a professor of philosophy at the University of Pennsylvania.

Cailliet's book *Journey into Light* has been a favorite of mine, for in it he describes the great mid-course correction of his life: his conversion to faith in Jesus Christ. The title says as much. He picked the title to contrast with Eugene O'Neill's *Long Day's Journey into Night*, because while it might be true that some in our culture were losing their vital optimism, Cailliet was in the process of finding his.

Cailliet, a French intellectual, had been raised with no knowledge whatsoever of the Bible or of Christianity. In fact, he had determined that he would live his life in total opposition to religion, to Christianity, and to the Bible. When he married, he told his young wife that there would be no faith, no religious literature in their home.

During WWII, Cailliet had seen combat, even been wounded. He wrote, "During the long watches in the foxholes I had in a strange way been longing—I must say it, however queer it may sound—*for a book that would understand me.* But I knew of no such book" (emphasis mine).

And so Cailliet set out to produce "a book that would understand me." He began an anthology of writings that would "lead me as it were from fear and anguish, through a variety of intervening stages, to supreme utterances of release and jubilation." In other words, Cailliet was going to put together his own private Scripture.

> The day came when "I put the finishing touch to 'the book that would understand me,' speak to my condition, and help me through life's happenings. A beautiful, sunny day it was. I went out, sat under a tree, and opened my precious anthology. As I went on reading, however, a growing disappointment came over me. Instead of speaking to my condition, the various passages reminded me of their context, of the circumstances of my labor over their selection. Then I *knew* that the whole undertaking would not work, simply because it was my own making. It carried no strength of persuasion. In a dejected mood, I put the little book back in my pocket." (Emphasis in original)

At the very moment that Cailliet reached this conclusion, his wife, in another part of the world, came into the possession of a French Bible and brought it home. Knowing her husband's antipathy for the Holy Scriptures, she reluctantly began to explain how she had gotten it.

"But I was no longer listening," Cailliet said. "A Bible, you say? Where is it? Show me. I have never seen one before!"

> She complied. I literally grabbed the book and rushed to my study with it. I opened it and "chanced" upon the Beatitudes! I read, and read, and read—now aloud with an indescribable warmth surging within . . . I could not find words to express my awe and wonder. And suddenly the realization dawned upon me: This was the book that would understand me! I needed it so much, yet, unaware, I had attempted to write my own—in vain. I continued to read deeply

into the night, mostly from the gospels. And lo and behold, as I looked through them, the One of whom they spoke, the One who spoke and acted in them became alive to me.

Cailliet continued:

> The providential circumstances amid which the Book had found me now made it clear that while it seemed absurd to speak of a book understanding a man, this could be said of the Bible because its pages were animated by the Presence of the Living God and the Power of His mighty acts. To this God I prayed that night, and the God who answered was *the same God* of whom it was spoken in the Book.

I'd call this a seeker in motion—a deadly serious seeker who becomes a follower. There began in Emile Cailliet's life a remarkable transformation of being. The hidden life grew and grew, and the character of Christlikeness that emerged in his life was beautiful to behold. The world of academia knew Cailliet as an expert on the thoughts of Pascal. But those who had the privilege of knowing him at "hidden life" level knew that he was a man who learned to walk with God.

This is what begins to happen in the life of a person who commits to following Jesus. The hidden life comes alive, and life-change is activated.

I have a shelf full of books that speak of how Jesus went about training people for service. Many of them are thoughtful and well written. But while I do not want to seem to be a splitter of hairs, I want to propose that Jesus was far more preoccupied with building the hidden life of man and woman than anything else.

I've called the hidden life *character*. Jesus set out to make certain people into (shall we say) Abraham-clones, people whose character was pegged to their faith.

176

I am absorbed by His effort. But my interest is not merely academic or historical; it is personal. The older I grow, the more I seek insight into the hidden life, the many dolls who make up "me" in the interior life.

As it did with Abraham, the mid-course correction of the men we know in biblical history as the disciples started with a Voice. But this time the Voice was seen. It came from the lips of One who was quite visible: God in the flesh, Jesus of Nazareth.

We have no record that any of the men whom Jesus initially called to His side were in serious trouble. They certainly appeared to carry all the bruises and warts of the tough world in which they lived. But the Bible does not dwell on possible bankruptcies, illnesses, broken marriages, or depressions. Those do not seem to be the things that drew the men to the Lord's side.

Some of them were obviously curious about what Jesus was saying and doing, and that would not be surprising for people who lived very common lifestyles and knew nothing of vital optimism, the hope of a bright future.

Once they'd been spectators, then they were seekers. It is not difficult to imagine them saying, "I have questions, and if the questions are answered, well, I could follow this man."

Two of the more interesting calls were those given to Simon Peter and Levi. Both were engaged by Jesus at their points of daily work, Peter in his fishing boat and Levi at his tax office. In Simon's case the call was encased in the language of his work, terms he would easily understand.

Dealing with the calling Voice of Jesus was no easy matter for Simon Peter. He weighed the character of Jesus and made a quick and easy contrast with himself. At once he knew that the Lord was out of his class: "Go away from me, Lord; I am a sinful man!" (Luke 5:8).

Scripture never tells us whether Abraham resisted the Voice in similar fashion, but it is easy to conceive that he did. Perhaps I can imagine it because I remember when my track coach took out a notebook and showed me what he intended for me to become. "Sir, I don't think those times are in me."

The Gospel writers were somewhat economic in their use of descriptive words and could be excused for thinking that Simon's reluctance to the call of Jesus was only momentary. But it would be a mistake to think thus. It is far better to presume that Simon struggled mightily with the invitation and responded to it at first with much uncertainty.

I don't think Simon Peter and the others ever saw that first call with the utter finality that we see it in hindsight. We have always been impressed that they pulled their boats on shore and headed off to follow Him. Perhaps for a day or two? There is really no evidence to suggest that on that day they made a lifetime decision to quit the fishing business and sign on for a life of apostleship. It sounds more like the call I heard from my track coach: "I'd like you to come down to the field tomorrow and work out with a few of the track men."

The call did not go out to men noted for their advanced learning or high moral reputations. We have no evidence that any of the men were particularly bad, although Levi and Simon the Zealot have to be considered men of doubtful reputation, one a tax collector and the other part of a political movement known for its commitment to violence against Rome. This Simon could easily have had a murder or two in his record.

This is the important point. The call of Jesus to these men had little, if anything, to do with anything visible in their lives and everything to do with their hidden lives, the "dolls," if you please, that lived within. Blend together the words of Jesus from all four Gospels and you will conclude that on the character level, there was no difference at all between the men chosen and called to be with Jesus and those at the temple with reputations for impeccable religious behavior. On the level of the hidden life, all were sinners in His sight. But only a few were prepared to acknowledge it. And those were the ones He selected for mid-course correction.

No volunteer ever made it into the tight community around Jesus. *All were chosen.* Those who volunteered seem to have come with qualifications and conditions. I'd like to follow, you can hear them saying, but first I must do this or that.

For the space of three years, the relationship Jesus maintained with these men had everything to do with character, the hidden life of motives, attitudes, affections, and focus. And how He worked on the development of their character is instructive because it will offer us insight into the development or modification of our hidden lives.

Elizabeth O'Connor writes:

> Whenever a person considers his inner work done, he goes into retirement. A gloom settles over him. Imperceptible as the decay in him has been, it begins to show now in the rigidity of his bearing. The hardening of life forces are reflected in attitudes and reactions to events on the outer scene. The death the Scriptures so often talk about describes an inner state.

The inner work of these men, once started, was never finished. And that's the way it should be for anyone seeking permanent mid-course correction.

Chapter 18

BUILDING CHARACTER

I have felt for some time that the hidden life of character is formed in two phases. The first comes in the first eight to nine years of life when we are most affected by the dominant community around us, usually made up of family and close friends. During these years, we develop habits and convictions that seem most compatible with the world in which we live. These become, for the most part, our default way of thinking and experiencing the reality around us.

We learn politics of relationships: how to behave in conflict, how to cooperate, how to resolve tough situations, how to work, how to conduct ourselves in terms of ethical and moral issues.

Then the second phase comes: generally, a remedial one in which we spend the rest of our lives correcting or compensating for those things not learned or experienced or for those things learned insufficiently.

My wife learned as a child to finish things, and she remains a passionate finisher of everything she does. For reasons I do not fully understand, I did not acquire the finishing instinct. My mother's family was made up of quitters, a relative once told me, and that has been a helpful hint to me. But it has meant that all of my life I have had to work out of the second phase of the development of my hidden life. I have had to deliberately resolve to finish things and drive myself by sheer discipline toward the finish line. Finishing is not an instinct for me; for Gail, it is.

It was the task of Jesus to build men who would reflect His hidden life of character. He would build on their strengths and rebuild in their areas of weakness. How would He do that?

HE TAUGHT THEM

First, *He taught them.* Day after day He opened his life to them through words. Students of the Gospels have calculated that Jesus spent literally months and months in seclusion with a small group of men (women appear to have been present also) talking through every aspect of the good news He'd come to represent.

"The knowledge of the secrets of the kingdom of God has been given to you," He said to the disciples, "but to others I speak in parables" (Luke 8:10). It was a frank indication that He was telling the disciples some things that others were not hearing.

Obviously, the teaching sometimes went in one ear and out the other and sometimes didn't even get into the ear. When He tried to speak of the future sufferings that went with His redemptive mission, the disciples tuned out. They could not adjust to the thought. It was not a matter of intellectual disagreement; it was a problem of perception. The purposes of God for His Son, Christ, made no sense from their frame of reference.

The teachings of our Lord did not take place in classrooms or religious buildings. It happened, as best we can tell, in homes, on roads, in the marketplace, and out in quiet, secluded places where there could be hours of uninterrupted dialogue.

These are the places where people are most likely to change. When what they hear is bonded to the reality of what they are living with every hour. Why we have come to think that hidden-life shaping happens best in a religious building confounds me. Biblical people should know better.

HE MODELED A WAY OF LIFE FOR THEM

A second form of character building came in His *modeling*. Jesus *was* and *did* as He taught. "Learn of Me," He said. The frame for such observation was the weak, the sick, the poor. His treatment of women, children, adversaries, and would-be exploiters was a constant lesson in character. He demonstrated patience, compassion, kindness, truthfulness, and purity in something more than words.

Children were brought to Jesus for the traditional blessing of the teacher. The disciples, operating from an old perspective that said their Master should not be bothered (without an appointment?), began to shoo them away. "Let the little children come to me, and do not hinder them, for the kingdom of heaven belongs to such as these," He said (Matt. 19:14).

And they had to watch Him radiate kindness to some of the weakest of society: the children. "When he had placed his hands on them, he went on from there" (Matt. 19:15).

HE REBUKED THEM

Character is built through *rebuke*, and Jesus did not hesitate to speak into the darkness of men's hearts with the light of truth. A rebuke is a powerful, concise statement that cuts like a sharp knife.

When the disciples and Jesus journeyed south through Samaria and were refused hospitality by a small Samaritan village because their ultimate destination was Jerusalem, some of the Twelve went ballistic.

"Do you want us to call fire down from heaven to destroy them?"

asked James and John, revealing instinctively vindictive character when they had feelings of rejection.

"But Jesus turned and rebuked them" (Luke 9:54–55).

A rebuke is not for the fainthearted. Skillfully offered, it goes straight to the hidden life and thrives there. A good rebuke remains perpetually active and corrects deficiencies of character over and over again.

We have no other information that might instruct us about how this particular rebuke was received. I find it interesting that John, a man who would later be deeply associated with the theme of love and forgiveness, in this instance exhibited such an ugly spirit. I find myself wondering if this was the moment of John's great turnabout in character. Was Jesus' rebuke to James and John so sharp and incisive that they were never the same again? Possibly.

Some years ago I had the opportunity to share a hotel room in Thailand for seven days with the late Dr. Christy Wilson. I believe that anyone who has ever known Dr. Wilson will attest that he was a man of supreme Christlike character. And I saw that in action during the days I spent with him.

We were attending a conference on world evangelization where men and women from virtually every nation were gathered at the same hotel. Having arrived at the hotel late at night, we had gone straight to bed. Only in the morning when the sun had risen did we learn what sort of a view we had outside our hotel room windows.

The hotel was situated on the Gulf of Siam, and if the room was on the right side of the hotel, you had a magnificent view of the ocean. If the room was on the other side of the hotel, you had a view of an ugly dump and a parking lot.

I was the first riser in the morning, and when I opened the drapes, I looked out on the ugly dump and the parking lot. Without any thought, I said (this is character speaking), "Oh, no, we got the terrible view."

Dr. Wilson, just awakening from his sleep, was just as quick. And his words were both a declaration of praise to God and a rebuke to me: "Isn't that wonderful! It means that some of the brothers and sisters from the Third World who have so little will get a chance to enjoy a beautiful sight this morning."

A well-delivered rebuke lasts a lifetime and deals continuously with a part of character not made of God. So it has been for me. Almost never do I forget Dr. Wilson's words and his attitude when I feel the temptation to complain about something that does not seem in alignment with *my* best interests.

I imagine Jesus sitting down with the red-hot, highly insulted pair of brothers, James and John. They have been treated contemptuously by Samaritans who they've been raised to believe are their religious and cultural inferiors. I wonder what the Lord said? Did John have this moment in mind when he would later write, "He came to that which was his own, but his own [refused him hospitality]" (John 1:11)? How far had John come in the building of his own hidden life by that time?

Not long ago a young businessman included me on an E-mail distribution list when he sent a humorous "top-twenty" list to his friends. When I read through it, I could see why some would think it amusing. But significant portions of the humor had to do with sexual matters, excessive drinking, and (as far as I was concerned) general disrespect for women.

For a couple of days I wondered what to do with the E-mail. The sender was a man who has long expressed a desire to be a mature Christ-follower, a leader among biblical people. The easiest thing would be to ignore the E-mail, not to respond to it. Which is what I have done in similar situations on more than a few occasions.

On this occasion I couldn't do that. Somehow I feared that my silence would signal approval. What's more I cared for this man, and I believe in his future as a spiritual leader. Finally, I wrote, "I need to tell you that I don't think a man who wants to be in alignment with God's Spirit would send out a thing like that to his friends."

How would he respond? The answer came within a day.

His return E-mail read in part: "I'm sorry . . . rebuke joyfully accepted." A most suitable response.

If we cannot accept the rebukes that come from the community of biblical people around us, we can never hope to enlarge the hidden life. Character cannot be reshaped apart from the gift of rebuke.

I am not suggesting that we go about criticizing everything we see and hear in our brothers and sisters in faith, nor am I proposing that we heap to ourselves a weltering amount of self-criticism. But I am convinced that we should open ourselves, even ask each day, that the Spirit would send the occasional strategic rebuke into our hidden lives that corrects and enlarges.

Chapter 19

THE QUALITY OF LEADERS

HE BUILT CHARACTER IN THE CONTEXT OF COMMUNITY

Scholars have pointed out that nowhere in Scripture will we find Jesus alone with one of His disciples. Even the conversations that appear to have taken place between the Lord and one person were always conducted with others close by. If this is true, then we may have to question a lot of the so-called methods of modern discipleship, for it appears that Jesus engaged in character building when the "family" was together.

It occurs to me that one-on-ones (called mentoring) for the purpose of developing people engender a serious risk of creating dependencies and qualities of relationship that may not always be healthy.

I am not confident that we can ever learn the deep lessons of the hidden life of character without a community around us. The church congregation may be the beginning of this experience as it calls us to the regular exercise of worship and praise. We weary sometimes of the pettiness, the demandingness, and the unreality of which the church can be capable in its routine life. Surely, we say to ourselves, it ought to be better than this. But the church is family.

Community in its purest form may mean something deeper than even the average congregational experience. I speak of the small band of spiritual brothers and sisters with which each of us *must* have a covenantal relationship. Here we create a spiritual family built around biblical persuasions. We promise to live our lives in lockstep with one another, sharing the good and the bad, the joy and the sorrow, the blessings and the cursings of life.

I find much to think about in the words of Monica Furlong:

> Within the strange, sprawling, quarreling mass of the churches, within their stifling narrowness, their ignorance, their insensitivity, their stupidity, their fear of the senses and of truth, I perceive another Church, one which really is Christ at work in the world. To this church men seem to be admitted as much by a baptism of the heart as of the body, and they know more of intellectual charity, of vulnerability, of love, of joy, of peace, than most of the rest of us. They have learned to live with few defenses and so conquered the isolation which torments me. They do not judge, especially morally; their own relationships make it possible for others to grow. It does not matter what their circumstances are, what their physical and mental limitations are. They really are free men, the prisoners who have been released and who in turn can release others.

When first chosen by Jesus, the disciples had a long, long way to go before they could qualify under Furlong's definition of *community*: "free men, the prisoners who have been released." But the Lord brought them along slowly as He built in their hidden lives. And He made it quite clear what this meant when He said, "By this [your love for one another, your community] will all the world know that you are My disciples."

My life took a major step in depth when I regarded seriously the importance of biblically based friendships. My earlier books on the spiritual journey do not reflect an adequate understanding of the significance of community at all. It was only after I had known the ugliness of personal defeat in life that I understood the place of the community to feed into and place a guard on my character.

A year ago (from this writing) I was asked, along with two others, to engage in a very personal pastoral relationship with a person of some fame. My name was suddenly in the press and on television. For a while, my choice to do this was widely discussed, harshly criticized by some, kindly affirmed by others.

Several weeks into this experience, a member of my community came to me and asked if we could visit. "I have a question for you," he said. I invited him to ask it.

"In all this stuff that's going on, are you struggling at all with any kind of ego?"

For a moment I felt as if I were on holy ground. I had a friend who was committed enough to walk me into my hidden life and seek motives or attitudes that could be spiritually poisonous.

"I love you for asking," I said. "But I've really worked this through and I can assure you, there's no conscious sense of ego involved. But, please, keep asking."

The wisdom of Jesus is impressive. What He taught, what He modeled, what He delivered by way of rebuke became the property of the community, and it permitted them to enlarge their hidden lives together.

HE TAUGHT THROUGH MISTAKE
AND FAILURE

"I knew you had lost the race already," Marvin Goldberg said to me, "and I decided to let you lose it even though it might hurt the overall team." Like Jesus, my coach understood that failure is a master teacher if it has a willing student. He knew that few things ever gain the attention of the would-be listener better than a moment in which there is humiliation.

Almost all of the great lessons on character I have learned have come through one form of failure or another. This always leads me to wonder why we in the biblical community do not have a more enlightened view of defeat or failure. The Bible is replete with stories of how God has spoken most powerfully into the lives of men and women after they have sunk to the bottom. Why, after all of our appreciation of the meaning of grace, do we not have a better appreciation of what to do for the person who has failed in one way or another and has a chance to rebound in strength of hidden person?

Let's see: How many times did the disciples learn things through mistakes? Let me count the ways. There were the repeated times they resented the intrusions of the very people Jesus said He'd come to serve. There was their inability to understand the difference between the dogma of the temple and the perspectives of Jesus. There was their panic on the lake of Galilee during the storm that caused Jesus to ask them where their faith was.

What of their intrafraternal squabbling over who was the greatest? Or what of James and John (mother included) seeking positions of power or honor at the right hand of the Lord? There was, of course, the dishonorable performance of the Twelve on the night of our Lord's death. Promises broken, uncontrolled fear, betrayal, the stultifying doubt that caused them to instantly abandon all their dreams and trust in Christ when He was pronounced dead, even though He'd warned them about what would happen.

I shall always be appreciative for Jesus' warning to Simon Peter on the night of the Last Supper: "Simon, Satan has asked to sift you as wheat. But I have prayed for you, Simon, that your faith may not fail.

And when you have turned back, strengthen your brothers" (Luke 22:32).

I hear overtones of that strange and mysterious Older Testament dialogue between God and Satan in which the devil says, "Stretch out your hand and strike everything he has, and he will surely curse you to your face" (Job 1:11).

And so Satan sought a similar approach to Simon Peter. Given a jolt of pressure, Satan must have thought Peter would wilt. It all suggests that Satan was quite aware of the hidden life of this "first" disciple. Satan is a student of character.

Why didn't Jesus protect Peter from such a moment? To answer my own question, Jesus seemed prepared to look *through* the failure and on to the development of the hidden life that would come as a result. I hear Coach Goldberg's words, "I knew you had lost the race already, and I decided to let you lose it even though it might hurt the team."

A great English missionary leader of the mid-twentieth century Fred Mitchell wrote, "It is the quality of leaders that they can bear to be sat on, absorb shocks, act as a buffer, bear being much plagued . . . The wear and tear and the continual friction and trials which come to the servants of God are the greatest test of character."

The twelve men whom Jesus chose were not thoroughbreds. They were rough, shallow, easily intimidated people, not unlike Israel. But in three years Jesus built in their hidden lives, and when He finished, the character of the men and women who came out of His school became extraordinary. They would fit Mitchell's description of leaders.

HE SENT THEM INTO ACTION

Several times we read of Jesus' creating situations where the disciples would have to enter into ministry activity. While these are clearly training events, I believe character development is the actual priority.

These were times to learn how to draw on the power of God, to learn what their personal limits were, to learn how to speak into people's lives on levels they would understand.

The incident in which Simon Peter and John stopped along the way to the temple to address a man disabled from birth and heal him by heaven's power would never have happened if they had not learned to spot such people under the training of Jesus. They would have had neither ears nor eyes for him. They'd grown up moving past such people with haste; they'd now learned to stop.

"The practices during the week will be painful at times, but you'll come to learn that the race on Saturday will be a pleasure," the coach had said. And so Jesus pushed His men into practice. "Give them something to eat," He instructed His confused disciples who faced a crowd of several thousand. Is this a lesson in ministry methodology or a character lesson?

I vote for the latter. These are men whose hidden lives are limited by the humanly possible. They can operate only as far as they can see. And all they see is a small lunch good for one boy. The hidden life will have to be enlarged until it sees possibilities in conformity with great faith. No world-changing will come from men who cannot see beyond a box lunch. This is a day to have one's hidden life rearranged. To understand once and for all that biblical people have access to the God Most High whom Abraham learned to trust in the olden days on the mountain.

The character of a person is revealed in how he responds in moments of impossibility. The disciples showed their default character in the face of an overwhelming crowd. They would show a new kind of character when, later on, they would engage huge crowds in the streets of Jerusalem and preach fearlessly in the name of Jesus and call people to transformation. Their hesitancy of character was changed as Jesus pushed them more and more into difficult "practices" so that they could one day run the race with pleasure.

HE TAUGHT THEM TO
COMMUNE WITH GOD

Jesus rearranged the hidden lives of these men in one other way. He taught them the *devotional disciplines*. He showed them how to connect with heaven through the hidden life.

"Teach us to pray," they asked. And He did. He gave them a core prayer around which they could frame their own intercessions.

And then He Himself prayed, regularly communing with the Father. They often found Him out in the fields or on the mountainside praying. They were with Him (for a short time anyway) when He agonized before His Father in the Garden of Gethsemane.

They learned the devotional life through their own spiritual insipidness. A father with a demon-dominated son came to them asking for some kind of deliverance for his boy. Jesus was absent (up on the mountain—praying), and so they started in. But, nothing worked! As far as we can surmise, they said all the right words. But the boy remained captive to the evil demon.

Then Jesus appeared: "Jesus rebuked the evil spirit, healed the boy and gave him back to his father. And they were all amazed at the greatness of God" (Luke 9:42).

If you can think of the Master in a state of disgust, this is it. What other word could better describe His feelings when He says of their inability to pray this child out of bondage: "O unbelieving and perverse generation, how long shall I stay with you and put up with you?" (Luke 9:41)?

These are the disciples He speaks to. And then they ask a question that offers a ray of hope that something is happening underneath their thick skin: "Why couldn't we drive it [the evil spirit] out?" (Matt. 17:19).

I would once have been tempted to poke fun at this question, to suggest that it is a pathetic admission of impotence. But now I have affection for the question. I suspect it's the question of men whose hidden lives are beginning to hunger for growth and effectiveness. Finally, they are asking the right questions: How are we to pray? How many times shall I forgive? What does the story mean? When shall these things be? Where are You going? Why couldn't we drive the evil spirit out?

These are great questions, the questions of learners. They suggest men who have stopped pretending that they have their entire lives put together. They have opened up; they are hungry for the teaching, the rebukes, the modeling, the lessons that failure teaches so that their hidden lives of character may come into conformity with the Master.

In response to their question, Jesus tells them that they have too little faith. But if they had faith even the size of a mustard seed, they could move a mountain. And this can come only through prayer (Matt. 17:20; Mark 9:29). In such moments Jesus taught His men that the hidden life is enlarged only through the disciplines of the spirit.

"Now, Gordie, I want you to know that this is about much more than running times. It's about becoming a man. There are other goals far more important than these running times to think about. I'm going to push you to be a leader, to be faithful to your commitments, to keep up on academic discipline, to encourage younger runners, to grow in your Christian life. I am going to be tough on you, and there will be days when you simply won't like me. But if you'll stick with me, this is what you'll become."

The disciples (well, eleven of them) stuck with Jesus almost all of the time. Like in the summer when I sought to trash my commitment to my coach, they had their bad moments. Their worst? When they ran from Him in the Garden of Gethsemane and left Him alone to face His tormentors. They would never do that again. As it was for me, once was enough.

They never quit growing in the area of the hidden life after that. They became men of expansive character in whom the Spirit of God was pleased to dwell, and the face of civilization was altered as a result.

The many "dolls" within me sometimes are a difficult lot to control. Just when I think two or three of them are listening to me, a fourth and a fifth suggest something stupid. Slowly, however, I have come to believe that they can be brought into line, that they can find my hidden life a place in which they can all be comfortable. I like to think that as I am walking across the same ground as those twelve disciples, the many selves of Gordon are growing up to be like Christ.

AN AFTERTHOUGHT

We began this section with the stories of Israel. We ignored the occasional bright spots and bored in on those occasions when the darkest side of a people revealed itself. My purpose in being so selective was to demonstrate the appearance of shallowness when people live in virtual ignorance of the hidden life of biblical character to which we are called.

With some wonderful exceptions, Israel as a nation never stopped trying to build in the outer world. The people could not understand the words of the prophet who said,

> With what shall I come before the LORD
>   and bow down before the exalted God?
> Shall I come before him with burnt offerings,
>   with calves a year old?
> Will the LORD be pleased with thousands of rams,
>   with ten thousand rivers of oil?
> Shall I offer my firstborn for my transgression,
>   the fruit of my body for the sin of my soul? (Mic. 6:6–7)

All of these are *outer things*. The things seen, measured, assigned a monetary or human value. If the God of Abraham had been interested in the outer life of these people, this list would have been pleasing. But Israel couldn't quite learn that the Lord who had called first to Abraham wanted people of faith, of godly character, the kind of folk who would gladly walk up a mountain and surrender everything grace had given to them. Abraham was their model, but they never learned.

> He has showed you, O man, what is good.
>   And what does the LORD require of you?
> To act justly and to love mercy
>   and to walk humbly with your God. (Mic. 6:8)

These are the words of one who understands that the inner world comes first.

What Israel never figured out, the disciples did: That if you truly seek a changed life, you will *leave* in order to conform to the hidden purposes of God, and you will *follow* in order to revitalize the hidden life of Christlike character.

LIFE'S MID-COURSE CORRECTIONS
Flourish with a Commitment to Reach for the Highest Possibilities

Forgetting what is behind and straining toward what is ahead, I press on toward the goal to win the prize for which God has called me heavenward in Christ Jesus.

PHILIPPIANS 3:13–14

Be diligent in these matters; give yourself wholly to them, so that everyone may see your progress. Watch your life and doctrine closely. Persevere in them, because if you do, you will save both yourself and your hearers.

I TIMOTHY 4:15–16

Chapter 20

SHATTERING BARRIERS

Someone has collected a series of prophetic statements made by a few of history's smarter thinkers and leaders. They provide evidence that great minds aren't always reliable:

> Stocks have reached what looks like a permanently high plateau. (Irving Fisher, Yale, 1929)

> Airplanes are interesting toys but of no military value. (Marshal Foch, professor of strategy, France's War College)

> Louis Pasteur's theory of germs is ridiculous fiction. (Charles Duell, professor of physiology at Toulouse, 1972)

> 640K ought to be enough for anybody. (Bill Gates, 1981)

> I'm just glad it will be Clark Gable who's falling on his face and not Gary Cooper. (Gary Cooper on his decision not to accept the leading role in *Gone with the Wind,* 1938)

> We don't like their sound and guitar music is on its way out. (Decca Recording Co. in rejecting the Beatles, 1962)

The concept is interesting and well-formed, but in order to earn better than a C, the idea must be feasible. (A Yale business professor on Fred Smith's paper proposing Federal Express)

A cookie store is a bad idea. Besides, the market research report says that America likes crispy cookies, not soft and chewy cookies like you make. (Marketing experts to Mrs. [Debbie] Fields)

In my journals are any number of prophetic statements that I have made down through the years about the future that easily rival these for their stupidity and shortsightedness. I will be grateful if they never see the light of day. I apologize for the times I predicted someone's dream would be a failure. For the times I failed to see the potential in someone who seemed, at the moment, to be hopelessly awkward or naïve. For the times I could have provided the encouraging word but didn't because my eyes could not see beyond doubt into possibility. For the times I arrogantly questioned the sincerity of someone's repentance.

We can smile at some of the shortsighted comments and impressions of years back—now. But at the time, some of them could have had serious effects upon whoever was seeking a breakthrough in conventional thinking. What if, for example, Louis Pasteur had listened to Charles Duell and said, "He's right; why am I wasting my time looking for germs?" And every time we need to get an important document across the world overnight we need to be thankful that Fred Smith, founder of Federal Express, didn't listen to his B-school professor.

I came close to shutting down as a would-be writer when an important person in my young life laughed derisively at something I'd once written. I almost scuttled my engagement to Gail because a friend suggested that I might not have what it takes to be a good husband. To this day, whenever I am asked to offer a public prayer, I hear the words of a college girlfriend who said that my prayers were the prayers of an immature Christian.

Who knows how many ideas and aspirations, how many great works of art, how many attempts at new and resourceful leadership have been squelched because, at a key moment, someone planted doubt or discouragement in another's mind?

The greatest limitations, however, are the ones we clamp down upon ourselves. We permit failure, ridicule, age, or circumstance to inform our view of the future. We put our dreams away in a mental file labeled *Impossibilities*. We talk ourselves into the notion that we can never change, that we are stuck with who we are.

One day recently I decided to list all the potential fears that seek to paralyze me. My list, though not exhaustive, looked like this when I finished:

- That I can no longer keep up with a younger generation.

- That my mind has already produced its best thinking and that I have done my best work.

- That my usefulness to God is probably in its sunset phase.

- That I can no longer grow in my spiritual journey; that I am what I am.

- That my marriage will lose its vitality, and that my wife and I will become merely roommates instead of the lovers we are.

- That one of these days I will be stricken with a physical or mental disability and that my personal sense of freedom will be taken from me.

- That the rest of life will be same-old, same-old.

I will not permit myself to be captured by such thinking.

Many years ago, a good friend, Dr. William Wood of Emory University Medical School, told me the story of Ignaz Philipp Semmelweis, a Hungarian physician born in the early 1800s. At the age of three Semmelweis had lost his mother when she died while giving birth to her fifth child. Cause of death: puerperal or childbirth fever.

Perhaps it was the early loss of his mother that sensitized Semmelweis to the exorbitantly high death rate of women in childbirth. While others seemed to accept the fact that one in twenty birthing mothers died of puerperal or childbirth fever as a normality (sometimes the rate was much higher), Semmelweis found it unacceptable.

His vigorous clinical research suggested something we take for granted today: that the physicians themselves were most likely carrying the death-causing infectious substances on their hands as they moved from patient to patient on their rounds.

Semmelweis therefore concluded that "forced handwashing" with stringent solutions before and after seeing each patient would arrest the spread of disease. His conclusion was correct, and within a short time the death rate among birthing mothers on his service fell from 25 percent to less than 2 percent.

But the shocker in this story is that others in the medical community *refused* to accept Semmelweis's findings. For all the claims of scientific objectivity, their minds were closed to new possibilities. The we've-always-done-it-this-way mentality was as alive and well then as it is today.

The more Semmelweis insisted that handwashing was the key to stop the spread of infection, the more he was ridiculed and written off as a fool. Finally, he was forced from his position. When Semmelweis's successor did away with his handwashing policies, the death rate from puerperal fever rose from 1 percent to 40 percent.

Semmelweis died an early death, heartbroken over the refusal of the medical community to take his claims seriously. Forty years later Joseph, Lord Lister of Kings College in London, who was considered the father of antisepsis, would say, "Without Semmelweis my achievements would be nothing. To this great son of Hungary, surgery owes most."

My friend Dr. Wood writes, "There was a great reluctance to accept the facts of the case [of Semmelweis's findings] because it hurt the pride of an obstetrician and called for a change in his behavior."

Semmelweis was a *reacher*. Suddenly, I've introduced a new key word into this book. Watch it come alive: *reacher!* He was among the relative few who believed that a change could make all the difference and that change was possible.

As the years of our lives go by, we all have these moments when we entertain a wish to change our behavior. We meet a person who has disciplined his mind, and we admire his ability to deal with ideas. We are impressed with the coolness of a man under fire and wish we had his dignity. We see the tenderness between a husband and a wife and yearn that it would be so in our marriage. We sit, as it were, at the feet of a wise and godly man or woman who possesses unusual insight and wisdom, and we long that this quality might be ours.

We would like to break habits, alter personality traits, curtail anger, exercise greater self-control. We hate our proneness to envy and jealousy over what someone else has that we do not. We lack self-respect because we cannot master our sexual temptations. We complain about our busyness, yet seem unable to discipline the calendar. We wish we could be more selective about our priorities and less inclined to say yes to everything. We would like to know Jesus better, yet are forced to admit that too many other things come first.

What blocks the mid-course corrections that would swing us into conformity with Christ, with the person we, in our highest aspirations, would like to be?

Consider, first of all, *that it is more* typical *to love the status quo than it is to love change.* For all our protests that we would love to lose weight, something deeper within us (among the dolls) prefers the present habits of eating and sedentary behavior. For all our claims that we desire a quieter, more reflective life, something deeper within us (again, among the dolls) prefers the noise and the frenzied involvement of busyness.

Abraham never left Ur until he decided that he loved the promise of many sons in a far-off land *more* than he loved the familiar way of life in Sumer. *He had to cross the line from one love to another.* That's leaving!

The boomer who came to Jesus asking about eternal life may have been sincere. But Jesus forced him to see that he loved his acquisitions *more* than he loved what it took to seek Jesus' version of eternal life.

This is where the person in search of mid-course correction must begin. With an inventory of what is loved most. Our friends often know the answer to this question before we do. They hear what is most often raised in our conversations, what we spend our time and money on, what we are most likely to gravitate toward at choice-time.

A quiet day spent studying our calendars and (if we have them) our journals or diaries for the past six months will often inform us of what we love most. And when the answers come, they will be followed with a question: Is there something we love more?

Some days after the death and resurrection of Christ, a small group of disciples engaged in a night of fishing on the Sea of Galilee. Their efforts were fruitless. In the morning the Lord appeared on shore and filled their empty nets with fish. Soon the group was with Jesus over breakfast.

In the ensuing conversation, Jesus turned to Simon Peter and asked, "Do you truly love me more than these?" (John 21:15).

There are perhaps two interpretations of the question, hinging on what you think "these" means. Did Jesus refer to the fish, or did He refer to the other brothers at the fire? I think a sound argument might be made for either possibility.

"Do you truly love Me more than your business?" Or "Do you truly love Me more than your need to look good before your friends?" If Peter was to experience genuine change, he would have to decide what he loved more: the old, which too often held him captive, or the new, namely, the call of Christ.

This is Abraham's dilemma. Always the questions: Do you love

Me more than life in Ur? Do you love Me more than trying to preserve yourself in Egypt? Do you love Me more than carrying on business with Lot? Do you love Me more than your frantic attempts to obtain a surrogate son? And then the big question settled on the mountain: Abraham, do you love Me more than Isaac?

Bob Buford's book *Halftime* has brought enormous inspiration to many men and women seeking change in life. Buford's message is clear. There comes a time in a person's life when he has to decide that serving people offers more personal significance than adding more money to the pile. Buford speaks from experience. There came a day when he decided he loved building the kingdom of God more than building more businesses. And on that day, whenever it was, he underwent a dramatic mid-course correction.

A second thing that blocks mid-course corrections in many of us is *our fear of failure.*

What more needs to be said than that no one likes to appear the fool? We learn in our earliest years that failure invites rejection and derision. Before we realize it, we've permitted these messages to enter our hidden lives and cause us to feel devalued and inadequate.

Who knows what might have been driving the servant in the Lord's parable of the talents who buried the assets his lord had entrusted to him? When asked why he didn't do anything with what he had, he answered that he was afraid that he might make some mistakes, so he decided to preserve what he had.

No one knows, of course, where the story would have gone if the servant had said to his lord, "I studied the business scene carefully (here are my notes) and made some investments. But there was an unexpected recession, and I've lost your money." I would like to think that the lord would have said, "Your reward is as great as that of the servant who turned a profit because, in good faith, you took your best shot."

In the pursuit of change, we will likely taste failure.

My first attempt at ministry was a failure. I have never shaken the feeling that swept over me when I opened a crumpled piece of paper on the floor of a church room and read the words one of my people had written to another, "If MacDonald doesn't quit soon, this program will become a disaster."

I read the note several times and went to my office and wrote a letter of resignation to my supervisor. I was gone in two weeks. Soon after I was at work on the truck docks loading freight, typing bills of lading, and dispatching drivers. For a short while I thought that my entire call to ministry had been washed out in failure.

It was not the last failure by any means. I have failed in certain working relationships. I have failed to live up to an intellectual standard I once set for myself. Thus far, I feel as if I have failed to achieve the level of spiritual maturity I believe right for a man my age.

But I will not permit these failures to stop me from a continuing reach to grow and overcome the limitations my failures have disclosed. And I will not let others determine my course of life by their predictions that this or that will not work.

Israel was terrified of failure; so were the disciples. But the difference between the two communities was simple: Israel learned little from its failures; the disciples learned everything. They became a band of reachers.

Third, we are blocked from mid-course correction *when we resist the unknown.* No one ever set out to achieve substantial change of life knowing exactly what would happen.

Abraham headed for a land that was off his map. The disciples signed on for a remake of their lives, which had no precedent. As we shall see in the next chapter, the apostle Paul responded to a call that took him to the last place on earth he ever thought he would see.

The *unknown* can be intimidating. It demands that we learn new things, embrace new behaviors, adopt new attitudes.

Recently, the Washington newspapers told the story of the Sitowski twins, two women who were at the time of writing fifty-two years of age. For thirty-two of their adult years they remained at home caring for their parents. They rarely ventured from the home and lost touch with the larger world. Their parents have died, and the twins are on their own.

In an article titled, "Time Catches Up with Twin Sisters," Peter Finn wrote, "With the passing [of their parents], the hermetic shell around the sisters cracked to reveal an unfamiliar world that panicked them." The article continued,

> "I feel like we are in the middle of the sea on a raft, all alone, just drifting," Alice said. The sisters have no work experience to speak of and no friends. They have never taken a vacation, driven a car or dated and have rarely left their south Arlington (Va.) neighborhood on their own, they say . . . It means entering a realm they have not encountered before—a frenzied place of commuters, colleagues, bosses, computerization, paychecks and bills.

To put it mildly, the two women were scared of the unknown.

A younger generation finds commitment to marriage difficult because it means engaging in an unknown life and sticking with it. A man is afraid to let go of his job because he has no idea of what to do with his life once he sheds his title, his office routine, his working associates. I heard of a man who in seventy years of life had never left the state (not a large state either) in which he was born. The friend who told me about him said that he had driven with him on a trip that took him out of the state for the first time. "His whole body shook as he became aware that we were crossing the state line."

Here's a thought for you: We were meant to invade the unknown.

Jesus told Simon Peter: "When you were younger you dressed yourself and went where you wanted; but when you are old you will stretch out your hands, and someone else will dress you and lead you where you do not want to go" (John 21:18).

If Peter was something of a control freak, as they say, you can imagine what these words did to him. "Jesus said this to indicate the kind of death by which Peter would glorify God," John wrote. And then he added that the Lord said once again to Peter, "Follow me!" (John 21:19).

My friends Al and Marilyn Romaneski have spent twenty years exploring the unknown. Al was a high-ranking officer in the United States Army. When he retired, it would have been thoroughly understandable if they had returned to their New England home and cashed in on his military experience by landing a job as a highly paid executive with a local company.

Instead the Romaneskis decided to give themselves to serving younger military personnel at various bases in Europe. We have watched them move from one part of Europe to another, opening hospitality centers where military men and women, far from home, could find the love of Christ in the graciousness of their lives. When I ask who has reveled in exploring the unknown, the Romaneskis quickly come to mind.

Finally, we relinquish the opportunity for mid-course corrections *when we mistrust the Voice that calls us to life-change.*

In my earliest years as a pastor, there was a man in our congregation whom I greatly admired. He possessed remarkable skills when it came to making money. And long before he was forty, he had accumulated enough to assure long-term retirement from income production.

Almost weekly he came by my office and talked about how he felt a sense of call to leave business and engage in some form of Christian service. I am often leery of people who talk this language because I am not always sure whether they have heard a call or they are just anxious to leave a world of business that is tough on people.

In this case, however, I strongly felt that a man had been given a call. He had been prompted by God to *leave* his way of life and set out into the unknown. But when crunch time came, he found the leaving almost impossible. He loved the making of money *more* than he realized. But even more significantly, he was afraid that he didn't have enough money salted away to sustain his future life.

"I know God is calling me," he said. "I can almost hear Him telling me out loud that there is plenty and that He will provide." But he couldn't trust the Voice.

One day I was called to the hospital and watched him die. The seizure of his heart was totally unexpected, and he was suddenly gone when we assumed he had decades to live.

I have never been the kind to think that a death like that is linked to a problem of trust. But I will always remember my friend as a man who forfeited some terrific kingdom-building opportunities because he couldn't trust the Voice that called him to a life-change of service.

We are called to a life of *reaching*. To extend ourselves for the purposes of growth, service, a deeper knowledge of God.

Craig Barnes writes, "To mature as a follower of Jesus means to be led to the same powerless places He was led." Then he recounts an experience of listening to Henri Nouwen speaking to a group of theological students:

I can still see Nouwen leaning over the pulpit asking us, "Do you love Jesus? Do you love Jesus? Do you love Jesus?" He waited through a long pause. *Yes, Yes, Yes, of course I do.* I thought, *that is why I am here.* Then he made his promise: "If you say yes, it will mean meetings, meetings, and meetings, because the world likes meetings. It means parishioners who only want one thing of you, not to rock the boat . . . it means being subjected to endless déjà vu experiences. It means all of that. But it also means anxious hearts waiting to hear a word of comfort, trembling hands eager to be touched, and broken spirits with expectations to be healed . . . Your life is not going to be easy, and it should not be easy. It ought to be hard. It ought to be radical; it ought to be restless; *it ought to lead you to places you'd rather not go.*" (Emphasis mine)

Chapter 21

ALWAYS CONVERTING

In William Bennett's book of stories, there is a children's tale about a small gray mouse who lived in fear of an old cat. The mouse fervently wished that he was a cat. A fairy, so the story goes, heard his wish and transformed him into a gray cat.

Unfortunately, because he was a cat, a dog began to chase him, and he found himself once again filled with fear and wishing that he were really a dog. The fairy, hearing this second wish, orchestrated the shift, and the cat became a dog. But as the story goes, lions are attracted to dogs, and the newly transformed dog found something new to be afraid of.

"Please turn me into a strong lion," he begged of the fairy. Again the fairy, apparently something of a pushover, granted the request and made him into a lion. Unfortunately, it was soon hunting season, and a man tried to shoot him. Once more he ran to the fairy.

"What now?" she asked.

"Make me into a man, dear fairy," he pleaded. "Then no one can make me afraid."

"Make you into a man!" cried the fairy. "No, indeed I will not. A man must have a brave heart. You have only the heart of a mouse. So a mouse you shall become again, and a mouse you shall stay."

Instantly, he became a little gray mouse again and scampered back to his old home.

Here, in a nutshell, is the burden of this book on mid-course correction. Speaking out of the story: A life-change that offers the body of a man but the heart of a mouse is not a serious life-change. Biblical transformation begins with the heart and works outward. There is no other way.

Throughout this book, my effort has been to build on three words that overarch the journey of the biblical person. Three ways in which we respond to the Voice that is always reaching out in grace to those who will hear.

The first word is *leave,* a word graciously given to Abraham, calling him to a life of faith that was summed up in obedience, trust, and stewardship.

The second word is *follow,* again graciously given selectively to a group of men and women who formed the first circle of people around Christ. Theirs was a call to Christlike character, a transformation that would build them into men and women who were fit carriers of the good news to the ends of the earth.

But then there is this third word, *reach,* to become a reacher. It challenges biblical men and women to an ascending standard of life. Here, the word means to push yourself to something deeper, broader, higher, more enduring in the way of quality of soul and service. Reaching means embracing change. It calls people to the unknown and to the undone. It says never stop moving forward in both your inner world and your outer world.

In other books I have written of the day when General William Booth, founder of the Salvation Army, learned from his son, Bramwell, that a disease in his eyes would soon cause him to become blind.

"Do you mean that I am to go blind?" he asked.

"I'm afraid that we shall have to consider that, General," Bramwell said.

It is said that Booth was silent for a short while and then reached out to his son's hand and said, "For all these years I have served the Lord with my eyes. Now I shall have to serve Him and His Kingdom without my eyes."

Reaching is the response to the words the Puritan preacher Thomas Shepard used to say to his congregation: "Be converted and always converting." Reaching is the "always converting" part.

The greatest reacher in the biblical literature, in my opinion, was the apostle Paul. What accentuates his greatness in reaching are the obstacles he had to overcome to achieve his enormous sense of mission to evangelize his world. The man simply would not quit. No obstacle could stop him. And there were many.

"I came to you," he wrote to the Corinthians, "in weakness and fear, and with much trembling" (1 Cor. 2:3). Paul was well acquainted with the obstacle of physical weakness. His list of painful experiences in 2 Corinthians 11 is enough to make anyone wince. I am selectively editing his words when I recount them: I have worked harder . . . been in prison more frequently . . . been flogged more severely . . . five times I received the thirty-nine lashes [from the Jews] . . . three times beaten with rods . . . once stoned . . . three times shipwrecked . . . spent hours on the open sea . . . constantly on the move and in danger from bandits, from Jews and Gentiles, known danger in both city and country . . . been slandered . . . gone sleepless . . . been hungry and thirsty . . . been cold and naked . . . and besides all that, have lived with the anxiety that comes from worrying about the churches.

I have never heard anyone analyze what all of these experiences might do to the mind and body of a man over a period of twenty-five years. For myself, I can only speculate that one does not get away from all of this without scars—psychological scars as well as physical ones.

The one that catches my attention most forcefully is the thirty-nine lashes, experienced five times. It refers to a synagogue heresy trial that eventuated, if one was pronounced guilty, in a lashing of the bare back in front of peers. Scholars say that more than a few men died during this ordeal or later took their lives out of humiliation. Paul went through it five times.

Read Paul's description of those many experiences again, and read the phrases slowly and thoughtfully. Think of each event as a crisis in itself: life threatening, spirit disabling, schedule breaking. Most of us will never face even one of these events. But I am forced to ask myself, Would I have survived any of them? Would they have activated the quitter-gene in me?

This paragraph alone that describes the crushing moments of a man's life tells us how deep the original mid-course correction had gone into his soul and forged his mission in life. In another place Paul spoke of his so-called "thorn in the flesh" that, in spite of his prayers, God refused to remove. This mysterious disability, which has been the source of speculation for centuries, was obviously a serious drag for Paul. While most people think he spoke of a health-related matter, I have always wondered if Paul wasn't speaking of a character trait, say, an argumentative spirit that sometimes got out of control.

Witness his conflict with Barnabas over John Mark. That sounds as if it were a bitter dispute. Why couldn't Paul give in?

Whatever his thorn in the flesh, Paul found it a serious enough obstacle that he made three attempts to pray for deliverance. I suspect that we are hearing about long periods of fasting and praying. But the efforts elicited no response from God except the words, "My grace is sufficient for you" (2 Cor. 12:9). And Paul, like Abraham, settled for God's judgment. Surrendering to the hidden purposes of God, he concluded, "I delight in weaknesses, in insults, in hardships, in persecutions, in difficulties. For when I am weak, then I am strong" (2 Cor. 12:10).

I wonder why more preachers do not offer this as an instructive text for modern biblical people? It's the great teaching on prayer that comes up with a different response from what we bargained for. In a day when people assume that every problem has a solution, every question an answer, every malady a remedy, Paul is saying "not so" in his experience. But he is not thrown, his faith not shaken. The fact that this thorn (whatever it is) is to remain offers a new perspective to Paul. Rather than become resentful or doubtful, the man embraces the obstacle and chooses to squeeze an alternative possibility out of it. My weaknesses, His strength. You cannot defeat a man who thinks like this!

In any list of things that might have inhibited the reach of Paul, you have to highlight the sheer terror he must have known when adversaries set out to take his life. "We despaired even of life," he wrote from Ephesus where he was under constant threats of death from zealous Jews (2 Cor. 1:8). For almost two years during his stay in Ephesus, he probably arose from his bed each morning wondering if it was the day he would feel a dagger in his stomach or back from those sworn to take his life.

Anyone who has lived with a sense that death is close by knows what a devastating effect this can have upon the psyche. My only connection with the feeling came some time ago when I spent a week flying in a small plane from one village to another in the Amazon jungle (this was a different experience from an earlier story in this book). The landing strips were so narrow, short, and rough that I found myself terrified every time the pilot brought the plane in for a landing. The "male" in me would not let me tell anyone of my fear, but inwardly, I was scared that I was about to die. Each evening when we returned to the base, I would hasten to my room and write page after page in my journal. I wrote to my wife and to my two small children everything I could think of that they could read after they learned of my death. I struggled with a depression of sorts. I found it hard to concentrate. I counted the hours until I would leave that place and return to home where there was relative safety. I have never forgotten how deep the terror of those plane flights went into my soul in those days. And every time I read Paul's words about his terror, my mind snaps back to those days in the cockpit of a jungle plane. I understand what he is saying.

Still Paul, in the midst of his fear, would write, "But this happened that we might not rely on ourselves but on God, who raises the dead . . . On him we have set our hope that he will continue to deliver us" (2 Cor. 1:9–10).

Paul knew other kinds of weakness. He had *chosen* weakness as a way of life. "Men ought to regard us as servants of Christ," he said to the church (1 Cor. 4:1). This man who had been bred and raised to be a king in the world of organized religion, the smartest kid on the block, now referred to himself as a servant, in other places a prisoner. He deliberately took for himself some of the most humbling titles in his world. At one point he likened himself to an earthen slop bucket into whom was poured the treasure of Christ.

We must not underestimate the challenge this was for Paul. It is clear evidence of the mid-course correction that began on the Damascus road. The Pharisee of thirty-four years would never have written these words, never have thought these thoughts. It was not a part of his original wiring. But union with Christ had made a difference. The Savior with a servant's heart had given the Pharisee a servant's heart. Now, his mission was not to dominate but to serve. This is one big conversion of life.

In the writings that describe the life of St. Francis, a single line in the *Legend of Perugia* was brought to my attention in a wonderful little book by John Michael Talbot. "One of the most revealing snapshots of Francis's approach toward servant leadership," Talbot writes, "[is] hidden in a description of Francis's practice of traveling and preaching in churches. 'He brought along a broom to clean the churches.'" I can see Paul doing that.

Of course, Paul knew the weakness of sin. "What a wretched man I am! Who will rescue me from this body of death?" he wrote to the Romans (Rom. 7:24). With a mind toward total transparency, he acknowledged a darkness of heart that we all experience. But then contrasted against the darkness of the heart was the brilliance of Christ in him. "Thanks be to God—through Jesus Christ" was the answer to his own question about deliverance (Rom. 7:25).

So we have a man who has every reason to shut down on life. His body has taken a pounding; his mind has gone through a bitter hazing again and again. He lives in a world of adversaries who would rejoice at his death. He has chosen a life best described as that of a servant or prisoner. And he acknowledges an inner daily battle with evil that is as real as anything any of us face.

But these are not the only obstacles that might discourage a person from reaching. Toward the end of his life, Paul did, in fact, become a prisoner. From Jerusalem to Caesarea to Rome, Paul became acquainted with the chains that bound hands and legs. His freedom to travel, to shape his own calendar, was lost. Whatever control over his life he had enjoyed was gone. The limitations seemed to be progressively closing in on him, and there seemed to be no breathing space. Yet he wrote, "I press on" (Phil. 3:12). I reach!

As this book on mid-course correction nears its conclusion, I want you to join me in visiting that prison where Paul most likely came to the end of his life. I'd like you to hear him speak about how he handles life in the world he is in. This is a man who began life as a Jewish Pharisee, who was bred to be in charge. In his last days he finds himself in circumstances that are about as low as one can experience in the human condition. But watch him closely. This man is anything but low. He has been on a mid-course correction for thirty years—like Abraham. This prison is his mountain. And he is still reaching.

"We cannot anticipate or analyze the power of a pure and holy life," writes Francis Paget, "but there can be no doubt about its reality, and there seems no limit to its range in this strange and tangled business of human life, there is no energy that so steadily does its work as the mysterious, unconscious, silent, unobtrusive, imperturbable influence *which comes from a man who has done with self-seeking*" (emphasis mine.)

"A man must have a brave heart. You have only the heart of a mouse," the fairy tells the mouse in the tale that began this chapter. There was no mouse's heart in Paul.

Chapter 22

STILL WRITING POEMS

Some years ago, a Cuban journalist Armando Valaderes was arrested and held by Fidel Castro as a political prisoner. The conditions of his imprisonment grew steadily worse over the years as his guards tried to break his spirit. Valaderes would not break. At one particularly difficult time in his incarceration, Valaderes smuggled this poem out of prison:

> They've taken everything away from me
> pens
> pencils
> ink
> because they don't want
> me to write
> and they've sunk me here
> in this cell
> but they aren't going to drown me
> that way.
> They've taken everything away from me
> —or almost everything
> I still have my smile

the proud sense that I'm a free man
and an eternally flowering garden
in my soul.
They've taken everything away from me
pens
pencils
but I still have life's ink
—my own blood
and I'm still writing poems.

With little alteration, Paul could have written this piece during his prison days in Rome. Perhaps he actually said the same thing in a much more articulate way when he wrote to the Philippians about the conditions in which he was living.

No portion of Paul's writing in which he engages in self-disclosure moves me more than his first several paragraphs of writing to his beloved Philippian friends. As best we can tell, he is facing his last days; the possibility of execution is real.

In this letter Paul reflects upon three issues that I would like to call *reaching issues*. They may not be so universal that all of us face the exact things Paul had to live with, but they are representative of what we as biblical people are likely to encounter sooner or later. What characterizes these issues is that they force a decision: Will we give in to the logic that says stop, slow down, or will we reach beyond the moment to something greater?

In *Chariots of Fire*, there is a scene that has inspired me for several years. Eric Liddell has begun a race that appears to be much like a 400-meter event. In the first turn he is jostled and falls heavily to the infield grass. The camera zooms in on the prone Liddell, shaken for an instant and then alert. Everything slides into a slow-motion motif so that we can grasp every nuance of the situation. Liddell looks ahead and sees the runners rounding the curve toward the straightaway.

The question he must answer is obvious. After such a fall, does one bother to get up? Conventional wisdom suggests, call it a day. No one will blame you for quitting; you were fouled. The race is not important anyway. These are the reasonings of the inner voice that stresses limits.

But Eric Liddell reaches. Suddenly, he springs to his feet and sprints after the other runners, and before the race is over, he has passed them by and breaks the tape. You know by now that I am an ex-track man and will understand, then, why I thrill to this episode every time I watch it. The man *reached!* to his heart for courage, to his body for strength, to the situation in order to reengage it.

E. Stanley Jones, Methodist missionary and evangelist to the world (particularly to India), preached to millions during his nearly ninety years of life. He never retired. In his early eighties he suffered a serious stroke that left him unable to speak, hardly able to move. Yet he would not quit. He kept reaching. His last book *The Divine Yes* is one of the most remarkable of his dozens of books. Speaking out of his limiting experience that would have caused most people to lie down on the infield grass and remain there:

> I came to the conclusion that it had always been part of my life resources and my life plans to be taking up things that I could not do—and then by God's grace doing them. I never dreamed of a stroke that leaves you helpless as a call to present a Divine Yes, the universal Yes which meets a universal need. But perhaps it is in the fitness of things that it should be so.

Watch Paul reach in his prison situation when men less than he would have given in to the realities and called it a day: "I want you to know, brothers, that what has happened to me has really served to advance the gospel" (Phil. 1:12). This would have been a perfect chance for Paul to draw the attention of his readers solely to him and his predicament. Those who have never learned the discipline of reaching are most often tempted to turn the spotlight upon themselves: what attention they can achieve, what rewards might be theirs. This entire chapter looks at events in Paul's life that he could have used to capture the spotlight for himself. But on every occasion he chooses rather to look through the event and to see how it could possibly contribute to his sense of purpose or that for which he was reaching.

Blake's poem in which he speaks of the eyes is thoughtful:

> This life's dim windows of the soul
> Distorts the heavens from pole to pole
> And leads you to believe a lie
> When you see with, not through, the eye.

Blake understands the difference between *with* and *through*. Those who see with the eye are people of the moment. They will not be reachers because they have no long view: what things can become, where God is leading through His hidden purposes.

Abraham began his journey seeing with the eye. He ended it seeing *through* the eye, looking at life and reality from soul-level where God could assure him, direct him, disclose to him wonderful words of life unknown to others.

Now it is Paul's turn. Here he is in a dead-end situation where all others would assume that it is all over. But Paul sees through the eye into the hiddenness of God's purposes, and he is not afraid.

Here are three samples of reaching.

REACHING FOR OPPORTUNITY

Whether Paul is in a small cell or under house arrest, the issue is the same. He has lost control of his outer life. Remember that this is a world traveler, a man who has gone everywhere at whim for more than twenty-five years. He knows the roads, the sea lanes, the cities and towns as well as anyone, I suspect. But now he can no longer move about because he is chained to a prison guard and not permitted personal freedom of any kind.

It would have been a perfect time to wallow in self-pity. And who would have blamed him? Doesn't a man deserve better than this? Doesn't Paul belong, at this time in his life, on a beach somewhere? Isn't this a time to back off? No, Paul elects to reach.

"I want you to know, brothers, that what has happened to me has really served to advance the gospel. As a result, it has become clear throughout the whole palace guard and to everyone else that I am in chains for Christ" (Phil. 1:12–13). The words suggest that Paul, the reacher, decided to turn his prison experience into a seminary. One smiles, thinking of a theological seminary on official ground, paid for by the very government committed to extinguish your message.

What seems clear is that Paul took a look around him and accepted the fact that he probably wasn't going to do much traveling. So if he could not go to the cities, he would take what came to him. Soldiers. Soldiers ordered to remain in his presence, perhaps chained to him, for hours at a time. What preacher wouldn't kill for such a congregation?

In the days when Soviet Communists were vigorously persecuting the Christian church in the USSR, a Russian evangelist was imprisoned for "religious activity." He wrote, "I was put in a cell with approximately one hundred other people after my first interrogation. Suddenly I understood why I was in prison."

Now watch the man reach:

Before going to bed I prayed, "Lord, it used to be so difficult for me to gather people together in order to preach your Gospel. But now I have no need to gather them. They are already here. Make me a blessing to them."

The Lord heard my prayer. Prisoners were coming and going

through this cell. In a short time forty people believed in Christ. I taught them to sing hymns and pray.

This clearly angered the guards who insisted that such activity stop. But it didn't.

The authorities finally found out what was happening and transferred me to a cell with hardened criminals.

Watch him reach again:

Precisely at that time, I received from my family a parcel containing bread, sugar, and clothing. When I entered the new cell, the criminals' eyes searched me. I took a few steps, set my bag on the floor, and looked around at them.

"Men, today I received a parcel. Maybe there are some needy among you. Divide it."

A tall, sullen fellow, probably their leader, approached me, silently took my parcel, and divided it equally among all of us. "Here, this is your part," he said, giving me a portion and returning my empty bag.

As a newcomer, I had to take the worst place in the cell, but the leader said, "For good people we have a good place. Now tell us why they transferred you to this cell."

"Well in Cell 44 I taught people how to pray to God. The authorities did not like it, so they threw me in here."

The leader smiled for the first time. "Very good! Now you will teach us."

Paul lives! Perhaps I speculate too wildly, but I think of all the guards who entered Paul's circle of influence in that prison. I wonder how many of them heard the Voice all upon them to leave a pagan way of life and follow Christ? I wonder how many of them, inspired by this remarkably resilient older man, began to dream of reaching in whatever way God purposed for them to do it? And through them, Paul reached far beyond his physical limits. For guards would inevitably travel to the farther reaches of the Roman Empire. And wherever they went, Paul's gospel went with them.

Paul took a prison and turned it into a launching pad for his vision of Christ to the nations. That is reach.

REACHING THROUGH ATTITUDE

The old apostle faced a second potential limitation. This time the situation had nothing to do with place, but everything to do with people. The Christian community in Rome was spotty at best in its handling of Paul's incarceration.

"Because of my chains, most of the brothers in the Lord have been encouraged to speak the word of God more courageously and fearlessly" (Phil 1:14). That's the good news. But there is bad news: "It is true that some preach Christ out of envy and rivalry, but others out of good will. The latter do so in love . . . The former preach Christ out of selfish ambition, not sincerely, supposing that they can stir up trouble for me while I am in chains" (Phil 1:15–17).

Who are these people who would do such a thing? And why are they doing it? Are they power brokers who seek to diminish Paul's influence so that they can enhance their own? Are they purveyors of a particular doctrinal slant on the faith who know that as long as Paul is in prison, he will not confront them? Are they just jealous? They remind me of a comment made by the late Malachi Martin: "History teaches that Christians are capable of behaving like people without any religious principles precisely in order to further Christianity. The words remain Christian; the actions are un-Christian. The total result is catastrophic."

How will the old man handle this slight? Will he be tempted to write a letter to the Philippians speaking of the nastiness of Roman Christians? I might be tempted. Aren't we all, on occasion, tempted to focus upon those whom we deem as petty, small, contemptuous? It seems satisfying for a moment to pontificate about their small-mindedness, for when we cause them to look bad, we in turn imagine ourselves to be the better.

This is a subtle trap for all people who seek a higher way of life, who believe in reaching. It would seem that our acceleration to higher things might be made quicker and easier if we highlight those who are perceived as being beneath us. We appear to be moving upward faster if we match ourselves against those who seem to be moving slower. Paul could have done this. Here was a perfect opportunity.

But he didn't. This man reaches. He reaches beyond attitude.

"What does it matter?" he wrote, reflecting on what happened. "The important thing is that in every way, whether from false motives or true, Christ is preached. And because of this I rejoice" (Phil. 1:18).

Apparently, you can make this man angry if you fool around with the integrity of the faith and cause others to become confused. Get out of his way. But if your goal is to hurt him, don't bother. The man will see through your efforts and perceive them through the hidden purposes of God. He will not get caught up in small stuff.

In the book *The Community of the Future*, there is a story of Shriman Narayan, a gifted and privileged young Indian man born into a Brahman family. After returning to his country from England where he had obtained a doctorate at the London School of Economics, he went to live for a short while to pray at the Sevagrahm Ashram, the community of Gandhi. It was his hope that he would receive guidance for his future work.

While at the ashram he was assigned, as was everyone else, to daily maintenance tasks. In his case, the assignment was to clean the toilets. Brahmans were never expected to do such low-caste work, and Narayan immediately went to Gandhi to complain. He said, "I hold a doctorate . . . I am capable of doing great things. Why do you waste my time and talents on cleaning toilets?"

Gandhi's response should make us all think: "I know of your

capacity to do great things, but I have yet to discover your capacity to do little things. So if you wish to seek my guidance and blessings, you will have to observe all the rules of the ashram."

Here is Paul, capable in the little things because his eye is on the big things. Little people doing small things will not capture a square inch of his mind. Even their pitiful attempts to hurt will be cast in a larger picture: God's love needs to be proclaimed in the streets.

REACHING TOWARD EQUILIBRIUM

There is a third reach in this great letter of Paul's. He reached for equilibrium. And as far as I can see, he achieved it!

The apostle, now in his sixties and thirty years a follower of Christ, knew that his death was not far off. In a world where life expectancy was in the late thirties, he was truly a very old man. When he wrote this letter, he had to live with the fact that any day, he could receive word that his case had been forwarded to the executioner. He knew it was possible that without warning, a Roman official might appear at his door with the dreaded words, "Prisoner Paul, come with me." At least that was what the summons to death sounded like when Dietrich Bonhoeffer heard it 1,900 years later.

How does one handle life under these conditions? How had Paul handled the reality of pending death when he lived in Ephesus under constant threat? And what did he remember from the day he was left presumed dead at the dump in Lystra? This man had lived with death for a large part of his adult life. What effect might it have on him now?

"I know that through your prayers and the help given by the Spirit of Jesus Christ, what has happened to me will turn out for my deliverance" (Phil. 1:19). This sounds rather ordinary until we understand what deliverance means for Paul. It does not mean getting out of jail in order to walk the city again. It could mean getting out of jail because he is on his way to heaven. Read on:

For to me, to live is Christ and to die is gain. If I am to go on living in the body, this will mean fruitful labor for me. Yet what shall I choose? I do not know! I am torn between the two: I desire to depart and be with Christ, which is better by far; but it is more necessary for you that I remain in the body. (Phil. 1:21–24)

I want to say to Paul, "Now say this again so that I don't miss anything. I thought I heard you saying that it makes little difference to you whether you live or die."

And Paul says, "Yes, that's exactly what I said."

"An explanation would be helpful."

In my fantasy, the man explains, "If I continue to live, it means a continuation of my service to people like the Philippians. It means I get to point more people to Christ, get to develop more people in Christ, get to plant more communities that will serve Christ. That's terrific.

"But if I die, I get to be with Christ for whom I've been living all these years anyway. Frankly, that's the better of the two alternatives for an old man like me. It's—how do you say it?—a win-win situation."

Win-win? I call it equilibrium. The sublime level for which one reaches (or ought to reach) all one's life. To that point in life where the dividing line between living and dying ceases to exist. There is something to reach for on both sides of the line, and life on either side is acceptable. It all depends upon His hidden purposes. It is a conviction based on the strength of the hidden life of Christlike character.

E. Stanley Jones writes:

I looked forward to a gentle descent into my nineties and perhaps beyond with nothing but gratitude for what God has wrought, for I have watched him do it rather than doing it myself. I had endeavored to be a faithful and humble witness to Christ in every situation. Then suddenly Bang! I found myself and my future apparently in ruins. My means of locomotion were shattered, and I could not recognize my own voice on a Dictaphone. The only hopeful thing said to me was that the brain passages which preside over the intelligence were not affected. Everything else had been changed.

But I said to myself, "Nothing has changed! I'm the same person that I was." By prayer, I am still communicating with the same Person. I belong to the same unshakable Kingdom and the same unchanging Person. Nothing has really changed except my means of communication with the outside world.

The glorious thing was that my faith was not shattered. I was not holding it; it was holding me. I could still put up my three fingers and say, "Jesus is Lord!" Everything was intact. I can honestly say I wasn't asking, "My God, why?" I could and I can face the future with him.

This equilibrium is, in my estimation, the absolute peak of the Christian journey. It is reached not by those who have lived passively, letting things happen to them, but by those who have taken the time to regularly set their hearts on eternity.

In 1914 Sir Ernest Shackleton and a crew of thirty set out to traverse Antarctica. But before they could reach the frozen continent, their ship became stuck in the ice and, after a time, was demolished. For almost eighteen months Shackleton and his men had to endure unspeakably hostile conditions while they waited for rescue.

Finally, Shackleton and two of the crew set out across the South Atlantic for South Georgia Island seeking help. It was a 1,300-kilometer journey in a small, open boat. And when they reached the island, it became necessary to cross its mountains; that in itself was an incredible feat. When Shackleton brought all of his men home safely, he was heralded as one of the century's greatest leaders. Of the ordeal he wrote,

In memories we were rich. We had pierced the veneer of outside things. We had suffered, starved, and triumphed, groveled down yet grasped at glory, grown bigger in the bigness of the whole. We had seen God in his splendors, heard the text that nature renders. We had reached the naked soul of man.

I read Paul into Shackleton's words. He had indeed experienced a mid-course correction in his life that had continued throughout the days of his life. And when he came to his last, he was in touch with his "naked soul." Nothing was withheld from the altar, not even his own life.

He and Abraham would have lots to talk about. I can see the two of them in conversation—dare I say—over coffee. I hear them talking about what made them willing, if necessary, to lay their best on altars: Abraham, his son; Paul, his life. Perhaps the two men recollect the moment when they heard the Voice. Abraham heard *leave*. Paul heard, I will show you what things you must do for Me.

And the two left: Abraham, his home country; Paul, his "home" way of life as a Pharisee. Everything that was familiar, safe, valuable. And from that point forward, it had always been a journey. Life had changed for them. Never to be the same. What an interesting conversation to listen in on.

A FINAL QUESTION

What makes a Paul (or even a Stanley Jones) think about his circumstances? Answer: hidden rewards.

At about the same time Paul had written to the Philippians, he was writing to Timothy, his protégé in the ministry. "I am already being poured out like a drink offering, and the time has come for my departure," he wrote.

I have fought the good fight, I have finished the race, I have kept the faith. Now there is in store for me the crown of righteousness, which the LORD, the righteous Judge, will award to me on that day—

and not only to me, but also to all who have longed for his appearing. (2 Tim. 4:6–8)

Like a lot of us, Paul was apparently a lover of athletics. He had been to the stadium and seen the runners compete. He had watched the winner climb the stairs to the judges' box and receive the crown that went with the victory.

I have always wondered if Paul had a secret fantasy to compete on the track. Who would blame him if he did think about these things in his idle moments? It is clear, nevertheless, that Paul understood that awards go to the winners.

And he was quite conscious that there were awards awaiting him in heaven. They were the hidden rewards that only heaven appreciates. In Paul's world, as in ours, there were plenty of rewards for the person who strove for honor on the battlefield, for wealth in the marketplace, for power in the Senate. Doubtless he saw, as we do, the people who lived in magnificent mansions and were squired about in impressive vehicles (then chariots, now Gulfstream jets). These rewards were visible, the longing of virtually every person.

But Paul had traded a love for visible rewards for the hidden ones. Hidden, that is, from the eyes of the world. But not from the eyes of heaven. For there the angels and the saints—the cloud of witnesses— all watch as the rewards are given. They come in the form of "Well done" from the Father and the crowns of righteousness whose beauty we can appreciate only when we join the heavenly community.

It has been many pages since we first thought of the *Apollo 13* astronauts out in space in need of a mid-course correction. We have looked at all sorts of people, ancient and modern, who had this one thing in common. A desire for life-change. And the ones who found it were those who were willing to leave the familiar, the comfortable, and to follow the One who promised change in the hidden parts of the being, and to reach for those qualities of soul that heaven would one day reward.

SUMMING IT UP

The desire to write a book like *Mid-Course Correction* came to me a few years ago. It sprang from a question that has dogged me for a long time: How does a person experience deep change?

I have always been drawn to the question because I spend an inordinate amount of my time with people who are in search of change. They have lived just long enough to see patterns of life in themselves that do not reflect what they wanted to be, what they hoped to achieve, or what they thought God might have wanted from them.

They see flat spots in their character. They acknowledge default attitudes, which control thinking and action. They find feelings deep in their interior wiring that go way back to moments of humiliation, failure, or abusiveness.

All of us, sooner or later, discover what I call *themes of sin* in ourselves: moods of spirit and behavior that keep erupting in the form of temptation. Then there are the desires and ambitions that, in themselves, are not always bad, but often so dominate our personal horizon that they shut out the greater desires and ambitions of Christian maturity.

So the question then arises: *Can one change?* Become a different, deeper, more dynamic person? Deep change!

I have been part of a Christian tradition—the evangelicals—that has no doubt, at least on paper, about that question. Key words in our vocabulary point to our belief in change: *salvation, redemption, transformation, hope.* And we tell great stories about change: Saul of Tarsus, Augustine, St. Francis, Wesley the evangelist, Newton the former slave trader, and (more recently) C. S. Lewis, Malcolm Muggeridge, and Charles Colson. In the more popular sense, we love the stories of athletes, entertainers, and business leaders who have come to faith. The movement is rife with rumors about this luminary or that who has supposedly "come to Christ." Perhaps one of the reasons we like these stories is that they affirm the decision for Christ we once made and make us feel that we're in alignment with significant people. I hope there are better reasons than that.

So our movement is quite familiar with conversions. But I confess that I question our understanding of *continuing conversion,* the spiritual journey that takes us from the Cross and prods us toward Abraham's mountain and Paul's prison cell where the evidence of deep change shows itself.

A great English preacher A. J. Gossip once wrote, "I am too old for anything to happen now. The branches are too gnarled to bend. Tug at them, and they do give a little, but they spring back again. My ways are fixed; my character is formed; the channels are long cut in which my life must run on to the end."

I have a lot of respect for Mr. Gossip and his lifelong work. But I reject his characterization of himself or of anyone else. He's just plain wrong. The power of God to change a person must not be limited or diminished by such an attitude. There is hope for transformation in every day.

I find myself engaged in too many conversations with people who call themselves Christians but who are quietly disappointed or frustrated with their experience. It's not working for them. The faith they have embraced calls them to life *out there* where the activities are. The programs, the meetings, the conferences, the projects. They hear incessantly about how they are to participate in changing the world, but they know that they haven't begun to see deep life-change in themselves.

Not long ago the secretary of the navy ordered what he called a two-day stand-down for the entire United States Navy. There had been too many accidents at naval installations and ships in a short period of time. His instructions were that officers and enlisted personnel spend two days reviewing all procedures and safety policies. As a result no one moved, outwardly anyway. An entire military service stopped what it ordinarily did, turned inward, and took a hard look at itself as a system.

I know I'm going to invite scorn when I suggest that it would not be a bad idea for the entire Christian movement to do the same thing. What if our people suspended all radio and television broadcasts, turned off all printing presses, and shut off the direct mail? What if we stopped asking for money, stopped criticizing all the systems and structures of the world, and stopped launching worldwide crusades? What if we just stopped talking and started listening for a while?

What if we did nothing but worship, think and meditate, repent, and seek a new understanding of what the Christian gospel really does call people to be and to do? Frankly, I don't think we'd be missed if we dropped out for a while. And we, and the larger world as a result, might be the better for it when it was over.

During such a stand-down, we might discover, like Abraham, that God is calling us to a much greater *leaving* than we had ever imagined. "Leave your country, your people, and your father's household and go," God said to the father of all who believe. People seeking deep life-change must wrestle with this word and wring from it every bit of meaning it offers.

Many of us are disappointed in our faith experience because we have not left. The past must be abandoned through confession and forgiveness, or we shall not get to the future. I have seen this principle in motion every time I visit Northern Ireland where Christians struggle to see a bright future because the mistrust and suspicion of the past cannot be laid aside. Their struggle has helped me to see my own chains to the past that are a bit more difficult to discern but that are nevertheless there.

A stand-down might offer a chance for us to calibrate how well we are *following*. And for that matter, *whom* we are really following. It is in following that the hidden life of character is formed and re-formed. Israel reluctantly followed, and its corporate character showed the result. The disciples followed more and more enthusiastically, and they became remarkably changed and dynamic men. By the way, it ought to be noticed that Jesus was not reluctant to call them to periodic "stand-downs" as He taught them the character lessons that would equip them someday to go on the road.

I fear that we are too often perceived as mean and angry people. We call ourselves a people of prayer and redeeming vision. But we are not known for these things by the larger world. We are too often seen as presenting an arrogant and self-righteous spirit. We might seek a revival in humility.

Finally, change comes when we become *reachers*. When I speak to groups of people and tell of the time in my life when I realized that I had become a visionless person, the room grows very quiet. Over and over again I get the feeling that I am talking to people who have lost their vision, who have forgotten how to dream about a future in which there are growth, achievement in kingdom purposes, and joy at the thought of meeting Jesus.

How much I love to paint the portrait of the *reaching* Paul, who in that prison cell forgot those "things which are behind." He renounced all rights to whine about circumstances, adverse people, and the fear of death. This man who had once worn the uniform of a

Pharisee embraced the present reality and squeezed every ounce of opportunity out of it. I am reminded of the comment made by one of America's great marine officers in Korea, "We're surrounded on all sides; we've got the enemy right where we want him." In this moment Paul, like Abraham and the disciples of our Lord, is our model of what deep life-change looks like.

Joel Sonnenberg is a young man with a modern story of this kind of life-change. He embodies everything this book is about.

On September 15, 1979, when Joel was two years of age, he and his family were in a car driving north on Interstate 95. Stopping to pay their toll at the Hampton, New Hampshire, toll booth, they were rear-ended by a huge truck. The Sonnenberg car exploded into flames, and Joel, trapped in a baby seat, was horribly burned. Had he not been pulled from the car in a heroic effort, he would have certainly died within a few more seconds.

Joel Sonnenberg was marked for life on that day. Burned over 88 percent of his body, he lost a hand and had to have his face rebuilt. He has spent literally years in the hospital in rehabilitation.

Aside from the unspeakable physical pain, there have been the social struggles. Joel's father talks of "adults . . . who come up to you and take their little children, pick them up, and . . . take their finger and point it right into Joel's nose and start laughing and say, 'Look at the monkey. Look at the monkey.'"

But none of this, the persistent pain and the social stigma, stopped Joel. Years later, when he entered high school, he became captain of the soccer team, the president of the student body, and the prince of the junior prom. Later, at Taylor University in Indiana, he was elected president of the sophomore class.

When you hear Joel Sonnenberg's story (as it was recently told on CBS's *48 Hours*), questions spring immediately to mind. Such as, How does a young man find meaning in all of this tragedy? The limitations, the loss of a normal life?

"If I did not believe in God, then I'm doing all this pain for nothing. If I did not believe in God, then all these surgeries that I have gone through and continue to go through, and all the pain and suffering that I will continue to go through is for nothing. It's for dirt."

I hear a young man who has learned to trust in the hidden purposes of God, who has accepted the notion that in the hidden life, strength and power are to be found, who anticipates rewards presently hidden but later to be revealed in great glory.

But there was an additional challenge to Joel Sonnenberg in this story. What to think about the man who caused this accident? The truck driver, Reginald Dort, had been charged with aggravated assault but had fled the country and disappeared. For almost nineteen years his whereabouts had been unknown. Plenty there to cause a man a lifetime of brooding hatred. Plenty there to captivate the mind with fantasies of vengeance and retribution. Plenty there to nail a man to the wall and keep him trapped for the rest of his life.

What of Joel Sonnenberg's attitude toward this man whose recklessness had completely changed his life? Is there bitterness? Does he desire to extract vengeance? Here in the life of one young man is the drama being played out in the larger world today. It reflects the question that people in our country face who have been victims of racism, oppression, abuse, crime, betrayal. It speaks to the issues in Northern Ireland, the Middle East, Central Africa, South Africa, and Colombia: the places where there have been long-lived hatred and violence. Can a man—can a people—forgive? Can they engage in the greatest of all *leavings*? The leaving of all those hate-filled feelings of the past.

"I give it to God," Joel says. "I think that's justice. That's what we've always known, our family, is to [give it to God]." This is but one example of where mid-course correction begins.

Nineteen years after that horrific accident, Reginald Dort was found, arrested, and brought to justice. In court Joel Sonnenberg faced this man who had caused him such pain and change of life.

"The earliest memories I have are growing up in a hospital," he said to Dort. "There I actually experienced every child's nightmare of being helpless. These memories continue to haunt me to this day."

As he neared the end of his statement—the victim speaking to the victimizer—Joel went on, "This is my prayer for you, Mr. Reginald Dort, that you may know that grace has no limits. We will not consume our lives with hatred because hatred only brings misery. Yet we will surround our lives with love, unconditional love in God's grace."

Wish he were someone else? Spend his time in regret, wondering what might have been? "This is all I've known. This is part of my being. And to be bitter about who I am? I am happy with who I am."

Joel Sonnenberg is only twenty-one years old. But he has already lived much longer than most of us—on a spiritual level. He has known the deep life-change, the mid-course correction, which comes:

- When a person learns to leave and journey according to the hidden purposes of God.
- When a person learns to follow and master the hidden life of character according to Christ.
- When a person learns to reach beyond circumstances, adversity, and death to the hidden rewards that lie waiting for those who enter eternity with Him.

Living like this brings mid-course correction of the deepest sort. And we shall not be disappointed.

BIBLIOGRAPHY

Barnes, Craig. *When God Interrupts*. Don Mills, Canada: InterVarsity Press, 1996.

Bennett, William J. *The Moral Compass*. New York: Simon & Schuster, 1996.

Bunyan, John, *Pilgrim's Progress*. I have taken the liberty of revising the original English of John Bunyan's *Pilgrim's Progress* into a more popular English of our day.

Cahill, Thomas. *The Gifts of the Jews*. New York: Doubleday, 1998. I am grateful to Thomas Cahill and his book *The Gift of the Jews* for influencing my attraction to Abraham as a model of faith.

Cailliet, Emile. *Journey into the Light*. Grand Rapids: Zondervan, 1968.

Colson, Charles W. *Born Again*. New York: Doubleday, 1995.

Hesselbein, Frances (ed.) et al. *The Community of the Future*. New York: Jossey-Bass (Simon & Schuster), 1998.

Jones, E. Stanley. *The Divine Yes*. Nashville: Abingdon, 1992.

Keegan, John. *The First World War*. Pimlico (Random House: London), 1999.

Lewis, C. S. *Surprised by Joy: The Shape of My Early Life*. New York: Harbrace, 1966.

Nouwen, Henri. *Sabbatical Journey: The Final Year*. Merrick, NY: Crossroads, 1999.

O'Connor, Elizabeth. *Our Many Selves*. New York: Harper and Row, 1971.

Patterson, Ben. *Waiting: Finding Hope When God Seems Silent*. Don Mills, Canada: InterVarsity Press, 1990.

Snyder, Don. *Cliff Walk*. New York: Little Brown, 1998.

Vallederes, Armando. *Against All Hope*. New York: Knopf, 1980.

Willimon, William H. *The Intrusive Word*. Grand Rapids: Eerdmans, 1994.

Wouk, Herman. *This Is My God*. New York: Little, Brown, 1992.

ABOUT THE AUTHOR

GORDON MACDONALD is a Senior Fellow of the Washington-based Trinity Forum, author and speaker with almost 40 years in the ministry. He was senior pastor at Grace Chapel, Lexington, Massachusetts, for 19 years, ministering to more than 3,000 each weekend. More recently he has assumed the role of Pastor Emeritus.

MacDonald has written many books and co-authored others with his wife, Gail. His most popular book is *Ordering Your Private World*, which has sold more than a million copies and has been translated into more than a dozen languages. Among his other books are *When Men Think Private Thoughts, Rebuilding Your Broken World, Renewing Your Spiritual Passion,* and *The Life God Blesses.*

As a speaker MacDonald addresses leaders' conferences in both the church and business arenas across the country, Europe, and Asia. He has taught or lectured at seminaries including Fuller Theological Seminary, Bethel Seminary, Denver Seminary, and Gordon-Conwell Theological Seminary.

The MacDonalds reside in New Hampshire and have two married children and five grandchildren.

Ordering Your Private World

This best-seller has already helped over a million readers find a sense of being satisfied from the inside out. By working through five specific areas—motivation, use of time, wisdom and knowledge, spiritual strength, and restoration—MacDonald gives readers helpful advice for fighting the disorder within and experiencing personal growth and spiritual development.

0-7852-7161-9 • Trade Paperback • $12.99 • 228 pages

Renewing Your Spiritual Passion

Gordon MacDonald shares many personal experiences with readers to pinpoint various problem areas that relate to spiritual exhaustion and mental fatigue. With this book, he helps readers recognize the areas of spiritual deficit and its causes and provides solutions for rekindling their passion for God.

0-7852-7162-7 • Trade Paperback • $12.99 • 240 pages

When Men Think Private Thoughts

MacDonald addresses the questions men often ask of themselves, exploring avenues that include sexuality and masculinity; intimacy, romance, and friendship; and achievement and definitions of success, revealing how each road intersects with a man's soul. Readers will be able to put aside the stereotypical definitions of maleness that plague men's private thoughts and will see instead a Christ-centered model. This book was designed for men, but will also help women better understand the men they love.

0-7852-7163-5• Trade Paperback • $12.99 • 288 pages

The Life God Blesses

MacDonald asks readers if they are prepared for the storms of life, or if they are more concerned with outward appearances than with what lies beneath the surface in their soul. Skillfully, he leads readers through the steps necessary to develop a mature soul and to recognize and receive God's blessings.

0-7852-7160-0• Trade Paperback • $12.99 • 276 pages

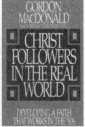

Christ Followers in the Real World

How do you take the enthusiasm and strength you feel at the end of the church service and make a difference with it during the week? In *Christ Followers in the Real World,* MacDonald reveals a practical four-step plan that will show you how to integrate your faith into the obstacle course of daily life so that you come over the hurdles a winner.

0-8407-9119-4• Trade Paperback • $12.99 • 240 pages